Y0-BSN-259

Field Guides to Finding a New Career

Sports Industry

The Field Guides to Finding a New Career series

Field Guides
to Finding a
New Career

Sports Industry

By John Greenwald

Ferguson Publishing
An imprint of Infobase Publishing

Field Guides to Finding a New Career: Sports Industry

Ferguson
An imprint of Infobase Publishing
132 West 31st Street
New York, NY 10001

Library of Congress Cataloging-in-Publication Data

Greenwald, John.
  Sports industry / by John Greenwald.
     p. cm. — (Field guides to finding a new career)
  ISBN-13: 978-0-8160-7997-1 (hardcover : alk. paper)
  ISBN-10: 0-8160-7997-8 (hardcover : alk. paper)
1. Sports—Vocational guidance. I. Title.
  GV734.3.G74 2010
  796.023—dc22

                    2010002345

Ferguson books are available at special discounts when purchased in bulk quantities for businesses, associations, institutions, or sales promotions. Please call our Special Sales Department in New York at (212) 967-8800 or (800) 322-8755.

You can find Ferguson on the World Wide Web at http://www.fergpubco.com

Produced by Print Matters, Inc.
Text design by A Good Thing, Inc.
Illustrations by Molly Crabapple
Cover design by Takeshi Takahashi
Cover printed by Bang Printing, Brainerd, MN
Book printed and bound by Bang Printing, Brainerd, MN
Date printed: April 2010
Printed in the United States of America

10 9 8 7 6 5 4 3 2 1

This book is printed on acid-free paper.

Contents

Introduction: Finding a New Career

Today, changing jobs is an accepted and normal part of life. In fact, according to the Bureau of Labor Statistics, Americans born between 1957 and 1964 held an average of 9.6 jobs from the ages of 18 to 36. The reasons for this are varied: To begin with, people live longer and healthier lives than they did in the past and accordingly have more years of active work life. However, the economy of the twenty-first century is in a state of constant and rapid change, and the workforce of the past does not always meet the needs of the future. Furthermore, fewer and fewer industries provide bonuses such as pensions and retirement health plans, which provide an incentive for staying with the same firm. Other workers experience epiphanies, spiritual growth, or various sorts of personal challenges that lead them to question the paths they have chosen.

Job instability is another prominent factor in the modern workplace. In the last five years, the United States has lost 2.6 *million jobs*; in 2005 alone, 370,000 workers were affected by mass layoffs. Moreover, because of new technology, changing labor markets, ageism, and a host of other factors, many educated, experienced professionals and skilled blue-collar workers have difficulty finding jobs in their former career tracks. Finally—and not just for women—the realities of juggling work and family life, coupled with economic necessity, often force radical revisions of career plans.

No matter how normal or accepted changing careers might be, however, the time of transition can also be a time of anxiety. Faced with the necessity of changing direction in the middle of their journey through life, many find themselves lost. Many career-changers find themselves asking questions such as: Where do I want to go from here? How do I get there? How do I prepare myself for the journey? Thankfully, the Field Guides to Finding a New Career are here to show the way. Using the language and visual style of a travel guide, we show you that reorienting yourself and reapplying your skills and knowledge to a new career is not an uphill slog, but an exciting journey of exploration. No matter whether you are in your twenties or close to retirement age, you can bravely set out to explore new paths and discover new vistas.

Though this series forms an organic whole, each volume is also designed to be a comprehensive, stand-alone, all-in-one guide to getting motivated, getting back on your feet, and getting back to work. We thoroughly discuss common issues such as going back to school, managing your household finances, putting your old skills to work in new situations, and selling yourself to potential employers. Each volume focuses on a broad career field, roughly grouped by Bureau of Labor Statistics' career clusters. Each chapter will focus on a particular career, suggesting new career paths suitable for an individual with that experience and training as well as practical issues involved in seeking and applying for a position.

Many times, the first question career-changers ask is, "Is this new path right for me?" Our self-assessment quiz, coupled with the career compasses at the beginning of each chapter, will help you to match your personal attributes to set you on the right track. Do you possess a storehouse of skilled knowledge? Are you the sort of person who puts others before yourself? Are you methodical and organized? Do you communicate effectively and clearly? Are you good at math? And how do you react to stress? All of these qualities contribute to career success—but they are not equally important in all jobs.

Many career-changers find working for themselves to be more hassle-free and rewarding than working for someone else. However, going at it alone, whether as a self-employed individual or a small-business owner, provides its own special set of challenges. Appendix A, "Going Solo: Starting Your Own Business," is designed to provide answers to many common questions and solutions to everyday problems, from income taxes to accounting to providing health insurance for yourself and your family.

For those who choose to work for someone else, how do you find a job, particularly when you have been out of the labor market for a while? Appendix B, "Outfitting Yourself for Career Success," is designed to answer these questions. It provides not only advice on résumé and self-presentation, but also the latest developments in looking for jobs, such as online resources, headhunters, and placement agencies. Additionally, it recommends how to explain an absence from the workforce to a potential employer.

Changing careers can be stressful, but it can also be a time of exciting personal growth and discovery. We hope that the Field Guides to Finding a New Career not only help you get your bearings in today's employment jungle, but set you on the path to personal fulfillment, happiness, and prosperity.

How to Use This Book

Career Compasses

Each chapter begins with a series of "career compasses" to help you get your bearings and determine if this job is right for you, based on your answers to the self-assessment quiz at the beginning of the book. Does it require a mathematical mindset? Communication skills? Organizational skills? If you're not a "people person," a job requiring you to interact with the public might not be right for you. On the other hand, your organizational skills might be just what are needed in the back office.

Destination

A brief overview, giving you an introduction to the career, briefly explaining what it is, its advantages, why it is so satisfying, its growth potential, and its income potential.

You Are Here

A self-assessment asking you to locate yourself on your journey. Are you working in a related field? Are you working in a field where some skills will transfer? Or are you doing something completely different? In each case, we suggest ways to reapply your skills, gain new ones, and launch yourself on your new career path.

Navigating the Terrain

To help you on your way, we have provided a handy map showing the stages in your journey to a new career. "Navigating the Terrain" will show you the road you need to follow to get where you are going. Since the answers are not the same for everyone and every career, we are sure to show how there are multiple ways to get to the same destination.

Organizing Your Expedition

Fleshing out "Navigating the Terrain," we give explicit directions on how to enter this new career: Decide on a destination, scout the terrain, and decide on a path that is right for you. Of course, the answers are not the same for everyone.

Landmarks

People have different needs at different ages. "Landmarks" presents advice specific to the concerns of each age demographic: early career (twenties), mid-career (thirties to forties), senior employees (fifties) and second-career starters (sixties). We address not only issues such as overcoming age discrimination, but also possible concerns of spouses and families (for instance, paying college tuition with reduced income) and keeping up with new technologies.

Essential Gear

Indispensable tips for career-changers on things such as gearing your résumé to a job in a new field, finding contacts and networking, obtaining further education and training, and how to gain experience in the new field.

Notes from the Field

Sometimes it is useful to consult with those who have gone before for insights and advice. "Notes from the Field" presents interviews with career-changers, presenting motivations and methods that you can identify with.

Further Resources

Finally, we give a list of "expedition outfitters" to provide you with further resources and trade resources.

Make the Most of Your Journey

Sports are a way of life for countless Americans. Millions grow up playing sports and remain passionately involved as fans and participants. Estimates of American consumer and commercial spending on sports top $400 billion a year for everything from game tickets to tennis rackets.

The love of sports is a legacy passed down through ages. Long before the first Greek Olympiad in 776 B.C.E., ancient Egyptian murals portrayed acrobats, ball players, and wrestlers. In pre-Columbian North America, Native Americans played a ball game that gave rise to lacrosse. More recently, President Barack Obama urged his fellow Americans to make "physical activity, fitness, and sports participation an important part of their daily lives."

The world of athletics offers many opportunities for people to turn their passion for sports into a vocation. Behind the players on the field stand legions of individuals whose time, energy, and expertise are an essential part of the game. Whether they are coaches or umpires who play highly visible roles, or stadium or equipment managers who go largely unseen, these individuals share in the excitement of sports and are crucial to making sporting events happen. Career changers have plenty of ways to enter such lines of work. By networking and matching their skills to available occupations, even people who have never played sports or studied them in college can land good jobs with prospects for advancement.

The process of job advancement in the field of sports is often said to be shaped like a pyramid: at the wide base are many jobs with youth or high school athletic teams, while at the narrow tip are the few, highly coveted jobs with professional organizations. Thus there are many sports jobs altogether, but the competition becomes increasingly tough as one works his or her way up. The salaries of various positions reflect this pyramid model. For example, high school football and basketball coaches are typically teachers who get paid a little extra for their after-class work. But coaches of the same sports at big universities can become national celebrities who earn more than $1 million a year before endorsements, dwarfing the salaries of college presidents. One notch higher up are the National Football League and the National Basketball

Association, where head coaches can earn many times more than their best-paid campus counterparts.

Referees and umpires face a similar climb. While referees who work high school football games are part-timers who are paid relatively little, veteran NFL officials can earn six-figure salaries. However, it may take 20 years of experience before a referee can begin to work NFL games. Even college and university sports have levels. The National Collegiate Athletic Association groups schools into three divisions ranging from Division I at the highest level to Division III at the lowest, based on the number of athletic scholarships awarded by the school. Division I itself is split into schools that are eligible to compete in post-season football bowl games, and schools that are not.

In fact, this dividing and subdividing starts the moment youngsters step onto a field in the presence of coaches and officials. Little League umpires, who are mostly volunteers, typically call balls and strikes for the youngest teams first and must work their way up to the Little League "majors." Only the best umps are allowed behind the plate in tournaments. Meanwhile, umpires who want to work real major league games must graduate from an accredited training school and toil for years in the minor leagues.

Many people begin their careers in sports by studying sports management and related topics in college. This can lead to undergraduate and graduate internships and the chance to make contacts and gain experience. An aspiring athletic director might then take an entry-level job in a college sports department and begin building a résumé by working in marketing and other areas. Former athletes can enjoy a head start in the race for jobs by virtue of their knowledge of a sport and their contacts. The ranks of major league baseball managers and NBA and NFL coaches are filled with retired professional players, for example, and ex-athletes often become scouts for teams and scouting organizations.

Yet because the field of sports is so vast and varied, career changers can break into it from many lines of work. The trick is to capitalize on the skills and experience that you possess. Although selling shoes or clothing might seem a long way from cheering football crowds, if you can help people find the right sizes and keep track of details, work in a college sports equipment department could be for you. Or if you are a teacher and enjoy helping students and want to try something new, becoming a coach or a fitness instructor might make good career choices.

Such skills can be valuable to an employer regardless of your age. If you are in your thirties or forties or older and have worked in advertising or public relations, sporting event managers could welcome you. Financial skills are always needed in athletic directors' offices, and anyone who has negotiated a contract has experience that sports agents can use. The biggest limitation that age may impose is on prospects for advancement. You naturally stand a better chance of becoming an athletic director or running a sports-equipment office if you start early enough to gain the experience and contacts you need to get ahead. But there is no cut-off age at which this becomes impossible. Meanwhile, past experience can serve as a guide to your future career. Some of the people you will meet in this book looked back in order to look ahead. A commodities trader who officiated lacrosse matches in college walked away from his job to attend umpire school. A marketing manager with a passion for exercise decided to become a fitness instructor. A former high school teacher with a love for baseball now works as a major league scout.

Networking is crucial to breaking into any field. You may already have valuable contacts among your coworkers, clients, or friends. Some sports agents began their careers by representing athletes they knew in college, or clients they had first advised as lawyers. If you work for an architectural firm or construction contractor, you may know a sports-facility manager who can update you about job openings in that line of work. Career changers have numerous opportunities to network. Colleges and private groups sponsor summer camps for young athletes, for example, giving aspiring coaches the chance to meet other coaches and do part-time work. Prospective scouts can make contacts at camps as well. Some scouts first worked as talent-spotters for colleges and professional teams that used them to canvass local areas. Major league baseball makes heavy use of such individuals. Even seemingly closed institutions can open their doors to people with useful know-how and skills. While high school sports teams are mainly coached by teachers, outsiders are often called on to help. Someone who has run track, for example, might find part-time employment as an assistant high school track coach at virtually any age.

The opportunities for employment in the field of sports are as varied as the means of attaining them. In brief, athletic trainers are a vital part of every team, but one that is frequently misunderstood. Such trainers work with players in high school, college, and the professional ranks to prevent injuries and manage rehabilitation programs when injuries occur. Many trainers would prefer to be called "therapists" since their work revolves around health. The job requires a college degree in athletic training, and graduates must pass a national certification test before they are hired in most states.

People who play sports for fun and relaxation can turn to another type of trainer for help with their games. Enter sports instructors who teach weekend warriors how to improve their backhands, or take the hitch out of golf swings. Professional athletes who want to sharpen their skills make use of instructors as well. This kind of work can be rewarding for anyone who has played a sport and enjoys working with others. Jobs are typically available in parks and public and private recreation facilities.

The growing interest in physical fitness has boosted opportunities for teachers of yoga, Pilates, and other forms of exercise. Gyms and health clubs hire these instructors—known as fitness workers or personal trainers—to supervise programs for groups and individuals who want to get and stay in shape. Some fitness workers open their own studios. Fitness jobs are expected to boom as the U.S. population ages and health-conscious baby boomers strive to get and stay in shape.

Agents and event managers capitalize on the popularity of sports and the athletes who play them. By negotiating contracts for players and taking a cut of their earnings, agents share in athletes' wealth without ever stepping onto a court or field. Event managers plan and execute sporting events that attract crowds, media attention, and sponsorship dollars.

Since competition is the heart of sports, many jobs require the ability to think and act under pressure. This is true whether the task is calling balls and strikes as a Little League umpire, coaching a high school basketball game, or running the athletic department of a major university. Fans are vehement about their teams and demand winners, and are unforgiving about bad calls and poor management decisions. Even people who work behind the scenes can face intense pressure. Stadium managers must keep their facilities in constant good repair, for example, and meet deadlines to ready them for game-day operations and vast crowds.

Also essential for most jobs in sports is a deft command of details. You cannot organize events, scout players, negotiate contracts, or outfit teams with proper equipment without being highly organized and detailed-oriented. Nor can you be a good fitness worker without carefully planning and managing safe exercise programs and keeping track of clients' progress.

The hours for people in sports can be long and irregular, and jobs frequently require travel. Scouts are constantly on the road, as are college and professional coaches, and referees and umpires who officiate games. Most sports jobs are certainly not for homebodies who prefer nine-to-five schedules. But for individuals who are drawn to the world of sports, the travel and hours come as part of the action.

Thanks to Title IX of the Educational Amendments of 1972, jobs for women are increasingly available in high school and college sports. The landmark legislation mandates comparable funding for men's and women's teams and has encouraged the growth of women's athletics. Colleges and universities belonging to the National Collegiate Athletic Association, or NCAA, added more than 800 women's teams to their rosters from 1995 to 2004, according to a Women's Sports Foundation study of 738 schools. The biggest gains came in soccer, golf, and softball. More women's teams mean more opportunities for women to coach and hold positions such as sports equipment managers and athletic trainers.

With these thoughts in mind, you are ready to begin exploring the paths to a sports career. Your chief concerns should be how well a job fits your skills and interests, and how to enter the occupation you desire. This book is designed to help guide your journey to a worthwhile destination. As Hall of Fame baseball player Yogi Berra once put it, "If you do not know where you are going, you might wind up someplace else."

Self-Assessment Quiz

I: Relevant Knowledge

1. How many years of specialized training have you had?
   (a) None, it is not required
   (b) Several weeks to several months of training
   (c) A year-long course or other preparation
   (d) Years of preparation in graduate or professional school, or equivalent job experience

2. Would you consider training to obtain certification or other required credentials?
   (a) No
   (b) Yes, but only if it is legally mandated
   (c) Yes, but only if it is the industry standard
   (d) Yes, if it is helpful (even if not mandatory)

3. In terms of achieving success, how would you rate the following qualities in order from least to most important?
   (a) ability, effort, preparation
   (b) ability, preparation, effort
   (c) preparation, ability, effort
   (d) preparation, effort, ability

4. How would you feel about keeping track of current developments in your field?
   (a) I prefer a field where very little changes
   (b) If there were a trade publication, I would like to keep current with that
   (c) I would be willing to regularly recertify my credentials or learn new systems
   (d) I would be willing to aggressively keep myself up-to-date in a field that changes constantly

5. For whatever reason, you have to train a bright young successor to do your job. How quickly will he or she pick it up?
   (a) Very quickly
   (b) He or she can pick up the necessary skills on the job
   (c) With the necessary training he or she should succeed with hard work and concentration
   (d) There is going to be a long breaking-in period—there is no substitute for experience

II: Caring

1. How would you react to the following statement: "Other people are the most important thing in the world?"
   (a) No! Me first!
   (b) I do not really like other people, but I do make time for them
   (c) Yes, but you have to look out for yourself first
   (d) Yes, to such a degree that I often neglect my own well-being

2. Who of the following is the best role model?
   (a) Ayn Rand
   (b) Napoléon Bonaparte
   (c) Bill Gates
   (d) Florence Nightingale

3. How do you feel about pets?
   (a) I do not like animals at all
   (b) Dogs and cats and such are OK, but not for me
   (c) I have a pet, or I wish I did
   (d) I have several pets, and caring for them occupies significant amounts of my time

4. Which of the following sets of professions seems most appealing to you?
   (a) business leader, lawyer, entrepreneur
   (b) politician, police officer, athletic coach
   (c) teacher, religious leader, counselor
   (d) nurse, firefighter, paramedic

5. How well would you have to know someone to give them $100 in a harsh but not life-threatening circumstance? It would have to be...
   (a) ...a close family member or friend (brother or sister, best friend)
   (b) ...a more distant friend or relation (second cousin, coworkers)
   (c) ...an acquaintance (a coworker, someone from a community organization or church)
   (d) ...a complete stranger

III: Organizational Skills

1. Do you create sub-folders to further categorize the items in your "Pictures" and "Documents" folders on your computer?
   (a) No
   (b) Yes, but I do not use them consistently
   (c) Yes, and I use them consistently
   (d) Yes, and I also do so with my e-mail and music library

2. How do you keep track of your personal finances?
   (a) I do not, and I am never quite sure how much money is in my checking account
   (b) I do not really, but I always check my online banking to make sure I have money
   (c) I am generally very good about budgeting and keeping track of my expenses, but sometimes I make mistakes
   (d) I do things such as meticulously balance my checkbook, fill out Excel spreadsheets of my monthly expenses, and file my receipts

3. Do you systematically order commonly used items in your kitchen?
   (a) My kitchen is a mess
   (b) I can generally find things when I need them
   (c) A place for everything, and everything in its place
   (d) Yes, I rigorously order my kitchen and do things like alphabetize spices and herbal teas

4. How do you do your laundry?
   (a) I cram it in any old way
   (b) I separate whites and colors

(c)   I separate whites and colors, plus whether it gets dried

(d)   Not only do I separate whites and colors and drying or non-drying, I organize things by type of clothes or some other system

5.   Can you work in clutter?

(a)   Yes, in fact I feel energized by the mess

(b)   A little clutter never hurt anyone

(c)   No, it drives me insane

(d)   Not only does my workspace need to be neat, so does that of everyone around me

IV: Communication Skills

1.   Do people ask you to speak up, not mumble, or repeat yourself?

(a)   All the time

(b)   Often

(c)   Sometimes

(d)   Never

2.   How do you feel about speaking in public?

(a)   It terrifies me

(b)   I can give a speech or presentation if I have to, but it is awkward

(c)   No problem!

(d)   I frequently give lectures and addresses, and I am very good at it

3.   What's the difference between *their, they're,* and *there?*

(a)   I do not know

(b)   I know there is a difference, but I make mistakes in usage

(c)   I know the difference, but I cannot articulate it

(d)   *Their* is the third-person possessive, *they're* is a contraction for *they are,* and *there is* a deictic adverb meaning "in that place"

4.   Do you avoid writing long letters or e-mails because you are ashamed of your spelling, punctuation, and grammatical mistakes?

(a)   Yes

(b)   Yes, but I am either trying to improve or just do not care what people think

    (c)   The few mistakes I make are easily overlooked

    (d)   Save for the occasional typo, I do not ever make mistakes in usage

5.   Which choice best characterizes the most challenging book you are willing to read in your spare time?

    (a)   I do not read

    (b)   Light fiction reading such as the Harry Potter series, *The Da Vinci Code*, or mass-market paperbacks

    (c)   Literary fiction or mass-market nonfiction such as history or biography

    (d)   Long treatises on technical, academic, or scientific subjects

V: Mathematical Skills

1.   Do spreadsheets make you nervous?

    (a)   Yes, and I do not use them at all

    (b)   I can perform some simple tasks, but I feel that I should leave them to people who are better-qualified than myself

    (c)   I feel that I am a better-than-average spreadsheet user

    (d)   My job requires that I be very proficient with them

2.   What is the highest level math class you have ever taken?

    (a)   I flunked high-school algebra

    (b)   Trigonometry or pre-calculus

    (c)   College calculus or statistics

    (d)   Advanced college mathematics

3.   Would you rather make a presentation in words or using numbers and figures?

    (a)   Definitely in words

    (b)   In words, but I could throw in some simple figures and statistics if I had to

    (c)   I could strike a balance between the two

    (d)   Using numbers as much as possible; they are much more precise

4.   Cover the answers below with a sheet of paper, and then solve the following word problem: Mary has been legally able to vote for exactly half her life. Her husband John is three years older than she. Next year,

their son Harvey will be exactly one-quarter of John's age. How old was Mary when Harvey was born?
(a) I couldn't work out the answer
(b) 25
(c) 26
(d) 27

5. Cover the answers below with a sheet of paper, and then solve the following word problem: There are seven children on a school bus. Each child has seven book bags. Each bag has seven big cats in it. Each cat has seven kittens. How many legs are there on the bus?
   (a) I couldn't work out the answer
   (b) 2,415
   (c) 16,821
   (d) 10,990

VI: Ability to Manage Stress

1. It is the end of the working day, you have 20 minutes to finish an hour-long job, and you are scheduled to pick up your children. Your supervisor asks you why you are not finished. You:
   (a) Have a panic attack
   (b) Frantically redouble your efforts
   (c) Calmly tell her you need more time, make arrangements to have someone else pick up the kids, and work on the project past closing time
   (d) Calmly tell her that you need more time to do it right and that you have to leave, or ask if you can release this flawed version tonight

2. When you are stressed, do you tend to:
   (a) Feel helpless, develop tightness in your chest, break out in cold sweats, or have other extreme, debilitating physiological symptoms?
   (b) Get irritable and develop a hair-trigger temper, drink too much, obsess over the problem, or exhibit other "normal" signs of stress?
   (c) Try to relax, keep your cool, and act as if there is no problem
   (d) Take deep, cleansing breaths and actively try to overcome the feelings of stress

3. The last time I was so angry or frazzled that I lost my composure was:
   (a) Last week or more recently
   (b) Last month
   (c) Over a year ago
   (d) So long ago I cannot remember

4. Which of the following describes you?
   (a) Stress is a major disruption in my life, people have spoken to me about my anger management issues, or I am on medication for my anxiety and stress
   (b) I get anxious and stressed out easily
   (c) Sometimes life can be a challenge, but you have to climb that mountain!
   (d) I am generally easygoing

5. What is your ideal vacation?
   (a) I do not take vacations; I feel my work life is too demanding
   (b) I would just like to be alone, with no one bothering me
   (c) I would like to do something not too demanding, like a cruise, with friends and family
   (d) I am an adventurer; I want to do exciting (or even dangerous) things and visit foreign lands

Scoring:

For each category...

For every answer of *a*, add zero points to your score.
For every answer of *b*, add ten points to your score.
For every answer of *c*, add fifteen points to your score.
For every answer of *d*, add twenty points to your score.

The result is your percentage in that category.

Coaches and Sports Instructors

Coaches and Sports Instructors

Career Compasses

Here is the breakdown of what it takes to become a coach or sports instructor.

Relevant Knowledge of a sport (25%)

Caring about the development and personal growth of athletes (25%)

Organizational Skills to create and run successful programs (25%)

Communication Skills to teach teams and individual athletes to perform at peak level (25%)

Destination: Coaches and Sports Instructors

Coaches are leaders, motivators, and masters of their sport, whose task is to bring out the best that their teams have to offer. Good coaches mold athletes into successful competitors by teaching them teamwork, sportsmanship, and fundamental skills. For men and women who love a sport and want to teach it, coaching can be a passionate and lifelong endeavor.

Sports instructors bring a similar attitude to the training of individuals. Instructors typically work one-on-one with athletes at tennis clubs, golf courses, swimming pools, and wherever sports are played. Students of sports instructors range from beginners to professional athletes who want to improve their game. Instructors share with coaches a devotion to a sport and a desire to teach it, as well as concern for an athlete's health and safety. But unlike coaches, instructors do not supervise competition: The instructor's role ends when the game begins.

For coaches of high school, college, and professional sports, game days mark the payoff of countless hours of practice and preparation. Coaches design game plans and keep teams focused as the action develops, while making changes and substituting players as needed. The final score indicates a team's strengths and weaknesses, and suggests what a coach needs to work on before the next contest. Keeping track of all this requires a keen eye for detail along with a strong sense of organization and the ability to communicate with players and others. Coaches and instructors need the patience and discipline to ensure that programs run smoothly and instructions are followed. Perhaps most importantly, work in this field requires a deep commitment to the personal growth of young athletes.

This is true at all levels and especially at universities, where coaching can become a 24-hour, seven-day-a-week occupation. Besides presiding over practices and competition, coaches must recruit high school stars, meet with boosters and alumni, and help team members over rough patches in their athletic, academic, and social lives. "It is more of a lifestyle than anything else," Fred Samara, the head track-and-field coach at Princeton University and former world-class decathlete, says of his job. "You may get a phone call from a student at three in the morning. You really have to love working with young people and understand the problems they go through in a day."

Given the enthusiasm for sports across the country, the demand for coaches and sports instructors is expected to grow faster than the average rate for all U.S. occupations in the coming decade. The U.S. Bureau of

Essential Gear

Let's go to the videotape. Coaches and instructors use videotape to teach athletes in every sport from Little League baseball to the professional level. Tape has many uses. By tapping an athlete's golf or tennis swing, for example, coaches and instructors can help the individual learn the proper technique. At the same time, coaches use tapes of games to analyze their team's performance and focus on areas that need improvement. College and professional coaches also use tape to scout opponents and view prospective recruits.

Labor Statistics forecasts that from 2006 to 2016 the number of jobs will increase from 217,000 to 249,000 in the category it calls "coaches and scouts," which includes sports instructors. Some 54 percent of the 2006 jobs were in educational institutions from elementary school through college, while another 15 percent were in categories that include recreational centers and professional sports.

Coaching may begin as volunteer work done mainly by parents whose children play sports such as soccer and Little League baseball. Little League coaches attend clinics and undergo background checks. Coaching as a paid occupation starts with school sports and is often an after-hours activity for teachers who collect extra pay for the work. Many high school coaches have bachelor's degrees in physical education. People who are not teachers but have bachelor's degrees may coach in some districts after obtaining a substitute-teacher certificate by filling out paperwork and passing a background check. Highly successful high school coaches may advance to college jobs. The median annual wage for coaches, sports instructors, and scouts was $28,340 in 2008, with the bottom 10 percent earning up to $15,530 and the top 10 percent making more than $62,660. However, professional coaches and high-profile coaches in sports at major universities can make million-dollar salaries.

Essential Gear

Know your playbooks and game plans. Football, basketball, and other team sports use plays that athletes must constantly practice. These can range from methods of attacking the goal in hockey to running passing routes in football. Coaches develop books of plays and drill their teams on them to prepare for competition. The plays are then organized into game plans for use against opponents. Similarly, sports instructors will put together lesson plans for students' courses of instruction.

Athletes just out of college can start coaching careers as graduate assistants. These are paid college and university positions that give newcomers valuable experience with all sides of a sports program. New graduates can also begin working as sports instructors. Many college coaches have played their sport and can draw on their experience to get jobs and build careers. Coaches in schools below Division I—the highest level—may be called on to coach more than one sport and to teach classes as well. Not until they advance to major universities can coaches focus on one sport as a full-time occupation. While some successful college coaches may break into the professional ranks, the competition is intense and opportunities can be limited. By comparison, sports instructors face a less strenuous career ladder. Many are athletes or former athletes who have been certified to teach at sports clubs and other recreational facilities. Instructors can build a following and go into business for themselves by opening their own sports camps or clinics.

You Are Here

Your journey begins with love for a sport and a desire to teach it.

Have you been an athlete? People who have played a sport may find it natural to go into coaching or sports instruction. They already know their sport and have established contacts that can help them land positions. Many high school and college coaches began as players. But non-athletes can break into the college ranks by starting in jobs such as equipment room assistant and moving up to assistant coaching positions when the opportunity arises. Prospective sports instructors with athletic backgrounds can work at a wide range of recreational facilities after graduating college.

Do you enjoy teaching? This is the crux of coaching and sports instruction. The job calls for helping teams and individuals develop by teaching in a patient and well-informed manner. Besides communicating basic skills, coaches need to impart the principles of fair play, respect for an opponent, and the importance of working together as a unit. Whether the task is coaching a football squad or teaching a tennis player how to serve, the end goal is always to enable people to enjoy a sport and succeed at it.

How organized are you? Coaches and instructors need to be highly organized to oversee teams and individual activities. This calls for discipline and the ability to keep track of details. For coaches it also means dealing with parents, alumni, and other interested parties away from the field of play. Coaches become the public face of their teams and should conduct themselves in an orderly and dignified manner.

Organizing Your Expedition

Before you set out, know where you are going.

Decide on a destination. What sport do you want to coach or instruct? Where do you want to do it? Most voluntary positions are at the Little League or other youth level. Paid coaching positions in schools below the ranks of major universities typically combine coaching one or more sports with other teaching duties and require at least a bachelor's degree. Full-time coaches work mainly in the major-college and professional ranks. Sports instructors have a wide range of workplace options that can be as varied as schools, health clubs, and ski resorts.

Scout the terrain. Good coaches and instructors are prized in every sport. Individuals can volunteer to coach youth sports by contacting league organizations. Most middle school and high school coaches and instructors are also full-time teachers, although others can get part-time

Navigating the Terrain

Where are you now? How will you become a paid coach or sports instructor?

Contact youth and recreational leagues for volunteer coaching opportunities

Earn bachelor's degree and obtain a substitute-teacher certificate

Seek position as graduate assistant or head coach in a high school program

Make contacts and pursue openings at collegiate level

coaching jobs by contacting local districts and obtaining credentials. For college and professional coaching positions, it can be helpful to have been an athlete. Sports instructors can work in summer camps and clinics while still in college and move on to year-round positions once they graduate. Instructors may need to be certified by organizations like the U.S. Professional Tennis Association for the sports they teach.

Find the path that's right for you. Anyone who loves a sport can coach or instruct it as an avocation or part of a teacher's occupation or as a full-time career. Those who begin coaching in middle school or high school are likely to spend their coaching careers there, although some may move to the college level. People with strong athletic backgrounds and an interest in college coaching can seek graduate assistant jobs that provide the opportunity for advancement. Experienced sports instructors can expand their practices to include professional athletes and may become entrepreneurs.

Landmarks

If you are in your twenties . . . With a bachelor's degree in hand, you can head straight for a job teaching school and coaching or starting work as an instructor at a sports club or other facility. If you played a sport in college now can be the time to seek a coaching position as a graduate assistant and begin building a résumé. A few gifted athletes may play professional sports in these years, or spend time training for the Olympics or other world-class competition, and look to coach when their athletic careers are over.

If you are in your thirties or forties . . . Look to attain your bachelor's degree and substitute teaching certificate if you have not done so already. If you are transitioning from outside the athletic field, think about what skills from your previous job may be helpful as a coach, such as leadership techniques or organizational ability, and highlight them when speaking with potential employers. Build up experience through volunteer coaching assignments with local, recreational teams.

If you are in your fifties . . . This can be the time for former athletes and others to take up part-time coaching jobs as a way of remaining active and working with young people. If you have significant experience

Stories from the Field
Craig Robinson
Oregon State University men's head basketball coach
Corvallis, Oregon

Craig Robinson has switched careers from basketball to banking and back again. Robinson, the brother of First Lady Michelle Obama, starred on the court at Princeton University and played professional basketball in Europe before taking an assistant coaching job at the Illinois Institute of Technology. He then put basketball behind him and earned an MBA from the University of Chicago Graduate School of Business. This led to a decade-long career in finance in which Robinson reportedly enjoyed a six-figure lifestyle. He went from vice president of Continental Bank to vice president of Morgan Stanley Dean Witter, then was managing director for the Chicago investment firm Loop Capital Markets.

Over time, Robinson gradually tired of the business life and hankered after basketball. He gave up finance to become an assistant coach at Northwestern University, whose head coach, Bill Carmody, was an assistant coach at Princeton when Robinson played there. After six years at Northwestern, Robinson became the head coach at Brown University and then at Oregon State, turning both teams into winners. Patience, discipline, and a deep knowledge of the game have enabled Robinson to coach successfully. His teams have benefited from the focus and strong work ethic that his years in finance helped him to develop.

with a particular sport, think about taking on clients to work as a sports instructor. Your life experience will be a highly sought-after commodity for potential students.

If you are over sixty . . . Similar advice for those in their fifties applies to you. Coaching is a profession that values tried-and-tested methods, strategies, and tactics. Seek volunteer opportunities and share your knowledge and lifelong devotion to a sport with your athletes. Remember that John Wooden, former head coach of the UCLA men's basketball team, won his tenth national championship at the age of 64, while Joe Paterno, the Pennsylvania State University football coach, has stayed on the job past his eightieth year.

Further Resources

The **American Alliance for Health, Physical Education Recreation and Dance** provides job listings, certification information, and online access to trade journals. http://www.aahperd.org

The **American Baseball Coaches Association** provides job listings and news and information about baseball coaching. http://www.abca .org

The **National Association for Sport and Physical Education** provides a wealth of information about sports and physical education. http://www.aahperd.org/naspe

The **National High School Athletic Coaches Association** provides information on high school coaching opportunities. http://www .hscoaches.org

Sports Official

Sports Official

Career Compasses

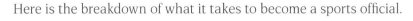

Here is the breakdown of what it takes to become a sports official.

Relevant Knowledge of the rules (50%)

Communication Skills to ensure that players and coaches understand the reason for calls and to resolve any conflicts that may flare during games (20%)

Organizational Skills to keep track of the action and keep games under control (20%)

Caring about accuracy and upholding the principles of fair play (10%)

Destination: Sports Official

If you like to keep order and can make split-second decisions under pressure, officiating at sporting events may be for you. Umpires, referees, and other officials are the decision-makers and rulebook enforcers whose word is law on the field of play, as this exchange among three umpires shows: "I call balls and strikes as I see them," said the first ump. "I call them as they are," said the second. "They're not anything until I call them," said the third. It is the last comment that most clearly defines the role of the sports official.

Such authority comes with heavy responsibility to match. Sports officials must be unbiased masters of the rules and imbued with thick skins. They must keep control of the conduct of games at all times, be good communicators, and stay cool in situations that can quickly grow heated—both on the field and in the stands. For every winner in sports there is a loser, of course, and the outcome may ride on a few crucial calls. Was that three-and-two pitch a ball or a strike? Did the football player cross the goal line before he went down? Was that last-second basket a buzzer-beater or not? While instant replay provides a fallback in professional and big-time college sports, officials at other levels are on their own. The stakes can be higher than just one game. High school athletes may hope for college scholarships, and key calls against them could hurt their chances when scouts are on hand. As one veteran high school official put it, "You never know who's in the stands."

Essential Gear

Familiarize yourself with the rulebook. Knowing and enforcing the rules with confidence is what officiating is all about. Each sport has its own rulebook, and regulations can vary from one level to the next. While there is usually no shot clock in high school basketball, men's college teams have 35 seconds to shoot and the time shrinks to 24 seconds in National Basketball Association games. Since rules may change from year to year, officials need to keep their knowledge up to date.

Making correct decisions takes concentration, good eyesight, and sound physical condition, as well as an ability to uphold the ideals of the game. Basketball referees race up and down the court along with the players and—unlike the athletes—get no relief from substitutes. Hockey referees streak across the ice to keep up with the action and must skate with skill. National Football League officials typically cover more than six miles a game. Officials who preside over youth and high school games teach sportsmanship and the value of playing by the rules. Consistency is a key educational tool: Fair play requires umpires and referees to apply the same standards to both teams when blowing whistles and making calls. Any hint of favoritism can anger players and fans and stunt an official's career.

Becoming an official typically begins as an avocation. Newcomers often volunteer to work Little League baseball games or other youth events. Volunteers attend clinics put on by Little League organizations and other sports groups that teach the rules. The next step for beginners who find the work to their liking may be part-time middle school or high school jobs. This calls for joining a statewide association for the sport of one's choosing, attending classes, and passing a written test. Standards can vary among different states. While some may require examinations for sports that are played at the middle school level, others may limit the test requirement to officials of high school varsity games. Breaking into the ranks of college and professional league officials takes patience, determination, and skill. Colleges hold tryouts that coaches can attend, and there is a big jump between small schools and Division I major conferences. For example, becoming a Big 10 football referee can take as many as 15 years from the time one begins at the youth level.

Essential Gear

Wear the correct field dress. Proper attire is a must, and officials below the professional ranks must provide their own. Uniforms should be clean and neat and comply with regulations. College hockey referees wear black pants, striped shirts and helmets, for example. Looking sharp is part of the game and adds to the perception that officials are in control. Many sporting goods stores carry uniforms for officials in addition to clothing and equipment for players.

For those umpires, referees, and other officials who do attain a paid position, the median wage and salary income is $23,730, according to the 2008 U.S. Bureau of Labor Statistics. The lowest-paid 10 percent of officials earned up to $15,450 while the top 10 percent made more than $48,310. At the same time, the relatively few officials who work in major-league professional sports can earn six-figure sums. Opportunities are expanding for officiating jobs. The number is projected to grow from 19,000 positions in 2006 to 22,000 in 2016 for a greater-than-average gain of 16 percent, according to the U.S. Bureau of Labor Statistics. Many of these jobs are part time.

Officiating jobs in professional sports are highly competitive. New National Football League officials may have more than 20 years of experience under their belts before taking the field. Candidates for professional umpire slots must attend one of two approved training schools whose curricula include five weeks of classroom and practical instruction. Successful graduates may spend up to 10 years in the minor leagues and survive a high washout rate before being considered for major league jobs. The process mirrors that of becoming a professional athlete: Many people start at the youth level but only a few reach the top. The satisfaction can be great for those who do.

You Are Here

Before umpires and referees can control a game, they must be in control of themselves.

Do you really want to supervise sports events? The challenges are many, but the rewards can be too. You will need a take-charge attitude, an even temper, and the ability to withstand abuse. Do not let yourself be buffaloed! Keep in mind that making calls on the field is far more demanding than second-guessing umpires from the comfort of your living room. But if you can withstand the pressure, you will have the satisfaction of serving as a role model for calm and effective decision-making, as well as ensuring that everyone plays by the rules.

Are you sharp-eyed and detail-oriented? Good officials see and interpret the action all at once. This takes complete attention to what is happening on the field of play and a thorough knowledge of the rules. Poorly prepared or inattentive officials do not last long at any level. You will need to steel yourself for tough calls and situations in which other officials may disagree with you, so be ready to stand by your decisions and move on. You must avoid the temptation to follow a mistake with a "give-back"—a compensating call to right the balance.

How enthusiastic and energetic are you? Sports are meant to be fun and officials are a key part of the games that fans come out to see. Umpires and referees should relish the opportunity to play their roles. Just as athletes burn off plenty of energy during a game, officials must be prepared to do so too. Not only must they move quickly to follow the action, but they must be prepared to fix errant buzzers, stuck time clocks, and other glitches, and to separate beefy athletes who square off to fight. They must also cope with overbearing coaches and fans and arrogant players, and remain enthusiastic while doing so.

Navigating the Terrain

I want to become a sports official

Contact appropriate youth and recreational leagues for volunteer opportunities

Gain experience in a particular sport, network, and attend workshops

Pursue openings officiating for high school, college, or minor leagues

Become a full-time sports official

Organizing Your Expedition

Before you set out, know where you are going.

Decide on a destination. Consider how high up the sports ladder you would like to go. Do you want officiating to supplement your income or do you hope to make it a full-time career? Part-time jobs are the most plentiful, and officials can increase their opportunities by working more than one sport. Someone who referees high school basketball during the winter, for example, might umpire baseball in the spring. Keep in mind that the starting points for part-time and full-time jobs are the same in most sports.

Scout the terrain. Youth leagues constantly need officials. Pick a sport and check the schedule for signing up volunteers. Get a jump by stepping up early and getting to know the organizers who assign umpires and referees. You will attend a clinic to learn the rules and how to position

Notes from the Field

Jeff Klinghoffer
Minor League umpire
Geneva, Illinois

What were you doing before you decided to change careers?

I was a commodity options trader on the floor of the Chicago Board of Trade. I traded options on fixed-income securities.

Why did you change your career?

After 17 years of that kind of stress I felt it was time for a change. I was healthy enough and competitive enough to do what I am doing now.

How did you make the transition?

My wife and I were watching an old black-and-white baseball movie called *The Stratton Story*. I had already been a college lacrosse official and my wife said, "Why don't you become an umpire?" This meant going away for five weeks to a professional umpiring school, becoming a top student, and then going away for another three weeks for an evaluation course. I told her that if this works out, I could be away for six months of the year. A 40-year-old had never done this before. I was 20 years older than the other students but it worked out.

What are the keys to success in your new career?

You can know going in that you are new and have a lot to learn. Find people to trust, that you want to emulate. Any job requires working hard, staying focused. The best bet is to learn from your peers who are accomplished in the field of umpiring. Emulate, learn, and listen. That is how I think you grow in this job. You need patience, a thick skin, and tremendous self-confidence. Everybody makes mistakes and when an umpire makes one he has to be able to shake it off and move on. There is no one to pat you on the back and say, "Go get 'em next time." There are sharks out there and you cannot let them know that you are not on the top of your game, because they will hop on you like nobody's business.

yourself on the court or field. Once you have gained volunteer experience, take the same basic steps to apply for high school and college officiating jobs. Learn all you can about sign-ups, tryouts, and clinic schedules and show up at organizing events. Even if such events are not specifically designed for officials, any contacts you make may prove useful. If your goal is to officiate professional sports, develop a strong résumé with years of experience. Network and keep a constant eye out for opportunities. Those interested in professional baseball can enroll in an approved umpire school.

Find the path that's right for you. A career as a sports official is built on knowing the game, the rules, and the people who organize and run leagues. Expand your knowledge in each of these areas by becoming a student of your favorite sport both on and off the field. The skill and enjoyment you bring to your work will guide you in the direction you want to go.

Landmarks

If you are in your twenties . . . Start building experience and contacts and develop your résumé. You will discover how much you really like the work and how well it fits your temperament. Those who have played a sport at some level may find officiating a natural move. Many prospective big league umpires enroll in an approved school at this age.

If you are in your thirties or forties . . . This is a good time to transition into high school, college, or professional jobs, depending on your level of experience. If you have children who play sports, seek opportunities to officiate in their youth leagues. One thing to avoid, however: presiding over games in which your own children are playing.

If you are in your fifties . . . Though most sports officials who are able to advance to major college or professional careers will have done so by now, this can be a fine time to take up officiating as an enjoyable avocation that helps to pay the bills. Remember that sound physical condition is a crucial part of this job, so make sure you are in good shape before seeking even volunteer opportunities.

If you are over sixty . . . Officiating enables you to bring years of accumulated wisdom and judgment to working with young people. Umpires and referees who exert a calm and reassuring influence can make games more enjoyable for everyone and are appreciated both on and off the field. Again, be sure you can handle the physical stresses of the task before taking up officiating as an avocation.

Further Resources

The **National Association of Sports Officials** provides a good overview of officiating plus online access to thousands of articles published in *Referee* magazine.   http://www.naso.org

The **International Association of Approved Basketball Officials** is a global organization that provides information on becoming a basketball official.   http://www.iaabo.org

The two major league-approved baseball umpire schools are the **Harry Wendelstedt School for Umpires** and the **Jim Evans Academy of Professional Umpiring**. Their respective Web sites provide information on enrollment, tuition, course offerings, and other topics.   http://www.umpireschool.com and http://www.umpireacademy.com

Athletic Trainer

Athletic Trainer

Career Compasses

Here is the breakdown of what it takes to be a successful athletic trainer.

Relevant Knowledge of the field (40%)

Caring about the teams and individuals with whom you work (20%)

Organizational Skills to maintain records of injuries and treatments and oversee rehabilitation programs (20%)

Communication Skills to keep players, coaches and others informed about a person's physical condition and treatment needs (20%)

Destination: Athletic Trainer

Athletic trainers are health professionals who work with sports teams and individuals to prevent and treat injuries. They should not be confused with fitness trainers, who are not health professionals and who train individuals to become physically fit. While athletic trainers are most often seen giving first aid to players who are hurt during games, this is a relatively small part of their jobs. The bulk of their job consists of working with physicians to assess an athlete's physical condition, develop injury prevention measures, and manage rehabilitation programs.

They focus on ailments of the musculoskeletal system—the joints, tendons, ligaments, and other parts of the body that are crucial to motion. Among the key decisions that trainers help make is when an injured player can safely return to action.

Athletic trainers work in a variety of settings, including schools, clinics, and professional sports teams. Employers can vary from dance troupes to factories where workers are susceptible to repetitive motion and related injuries. According to the National Athletic Trainers' Association (NATA), more than 50 percent of trainers work outside of schools. Whatever the setting, the job calls for detailed knowledge of human anatomy and physiology and of methods for treating acute and chronic injuries. It also requires a strong degree of empathy and communication, as well as administrative skills. Trainers may oversee their departments and should be able to recommend courses of treatment to players, coaches, and parents in a confident and reassuring manner. Familiarity with a sport or activity can help trainers relate to the people they work with. "I really understand where they're coming from," says Elaine Winslow-Redmond, who performed with the Radio City Rockettes before returning to school and becoming head athletic trainer for the precision dance troupe. Knowing the terminology of dance and the stress it can put on the body has been an important part of the job, she says.

Essential Gear

Study the book on human anatomy. Knowledge of anatomy and physiology should be second nature to people in this job. Athletic trainers must know the human body and how to protect it from injury and to repair the damage that occurs. Trainers cannot just rely on what they learn in school. To remain certified, they must continue to take medical courses to stay abreast of advances in diagnosing, preventing, and treating injuries.

New athletic trainers must earn a bachelor's degree from a school with an accredited training program that includes hands-on clinical experience. Courses range from basic and applied sciences such as biology and biomechanics to the prevention and diagnosis of injuries. In addition, nearly all states require graduates to pass a comprehensive national certification exam before working as trainers—46 states had this requirement in 2009. Some 365 U.S. colleges and universities offer accredited bachelor's programs, and many people go on to earn higher degrees to advance their careers. The NATA says nearly 70 percent of trainers have a master's degree or higher.

Athletic trainers combine a dedication to health care with an interest in sports and other activities. They work closely with coaches and consult regularly with physicians who give supervision. Physicians who offer guidance about injuries, treatment options, and related health matters also supervise trainers outside of sports. The trainers thus serve as both healers in their own right and as entry points to the rest of the medical community.

Athletic trainers in high school and colleges below the Division I level work with several sports teams throughout the school year. High school trainers may be called on to discuss preventive measures and treatment options with parents as well as with students. College trainers typically travel more and may put in longer hours because of team schedules. Trainers at universities with Division I teams generally focus on one sport. Like trainers at other levels, they evaluate athletes in preseason screenings, take note of any health concerns, and prescribe exercises or therapy programs for conditions that need attention. Trainers then work with teams and players throughout the season and may manage rehabilitation programs for injured athletes afterward. On professional sports teams, trainers provide health care on a year-round basis. Teams typically employ a head trainer and one or two assistants. All attend training camps, practices, and competitions, and work with team members before, during, and after sports events.

Essential Gear

Assemble a medical kit. Athletic trainers stand ready to administer first aid whenever teams step onto the court or field. Trainers must be thoroughly familiar with their kits and know how to stanch bleeding, clean and dress wounds, and when to treat injuries with heat or cold. Before the action starts, trainers break out their medical kits to reduce the chance of injuries. This can require taping and bracing weak ankles or knees, and fitting players with equipment such as goggles or nose guards for protection in games.

Trainers in clinics, hospitals, and similar settings treat and rehabilitate patients who suffer sprains, torn ligaments, and other athletic-type injuries. Such trainers may also work part-time in high schools and small colleges with limited staffs. In addition, the trainers may serve as community resources by conducting clinics and educational programs for the general public and other health care professionals.

The demand for athletic trainers is expected to grow rapidly in coming years, according to the U.S. Bureau of Labor Statistics (BLS). It estimates that the number of jobs will grow from 17,000 in 2006 to 21,000 in 2016, for a greater-than-average 24 percent increase. Reasons for the size of this increase include a growing participation in sports and other physical activities by people of all ages, and an increasing interest in health and fitness. Salaries depend on a trainer's education, experience, and level of responsibility. In 2008, the median annual wage for athletic trainers was $39,640, according to the BLS. The bottom 10 percent of trainers earned up to $23,450, while the top 10 percent made more than $60,960. Many top-paying jobs are with major college and professional sports teams, where the competition for positions can be intense.

You Are Here

Determine your interest and ability to be an athletic trainer.

Have you participated in sports or other physical activities? People who have played sports in school or recreationally have experienced competition and the demands it puts on the body. Even if one has not been a player, work as a team manager or trainer's helper can give insight into the health needs of athletes. Participating in activities such as dance, hiking, and bicycling also provides experience of the health risks of physical exercise.

Are you interested in science and medicine? Courses leading to a degree in athletic training are heavily geared toward physiology and related fields, and preventing and treating injuries. If you enjoyed biology or other sciences in school, athletic training could be a good occupation for you. Another measure of interest is whether you have studied or given first aid or cardiopulmonary resuscitation, since athletic trainers are typically the first medical responders when athletes are hurt.

Do you enjoy working with people? Relating well to others is an essential part of the job. Athletic trainers need to communicate with coaches, players, and health-care clients in a calm and reassuring manner that inspires confidence and trust. Athletic trainers also work closely with

Navigating the Terrain

Where are you now? How will you become an athletic trainer?

I have a bachelor's degree in a related field, such as biology

I do not have a bachelor's degree

Obtain additional training as needed to pass credentialing exam

Earn a bachelor's degree in athletic training from an accredited program

Apply for a position in a school, health care, or commercial setting

Seek out internships or assistantships while enrolled in school

physicians and other health professionals and should get along with them well. At the same time, trainers must cope with the stress of providing health care to highly competitive athletes, sometimes in the heat of hard-fought games.

Organizing Your Expedition

Before you set out, know where you are going.

Decide on a destination. Athletic trainers have a wide range of options when it comes to where to work. According to the U.S. Department of Labor, about 34 percent of trainers in 2006 were in schools, colleges, and universities, where they worked mainly with sports teams. Another 34 percent were in hospitals, clinics, and similar health care settings. An additional 20 percent worked in fitness and recreational centers. Other employers included professional sports teams, dance and other performance groups, and corporations that have expanded their use of trainers as a cost-effective way to prevent and treat injuries.

Notes from the Field

Chris Ryan
Head athletic trainer, Drew University
Madison, New Jersey

What were you doing before you decided to change careers?

I worked in back-office trade support for a Wall Street investment firm. Before that I worked in the Fulton Fish Market with my uncle who had a fish stand. I helped him unload fish from trucks and sell and deliver the fish to customers.

Why did you change your career?

I was pretty athletic and played lots of basketball and football in recreation leagues. I was always getting banged up and having knee and shoulder therapy and the work seemed interesting. When I had a herniated disk in my neck a doctor recommended surgery. But I preferred therapy and when the pain went away that proved to me that therapy worked. When I did my research, I found that athletic trainers work in schools taking care of athletes and that was the population I wanted to work with.

How did you make the transition?

I attended a full-time college athletic training program and worked part time to help support myself. I had some money saved up and also took out some loans.

What are the keys to success in your new career?

You have to have a sense of humor on the job because you often work crazy hours and it could be a stressful environment. Try to have a good time on the job. Empathy is important—you must empathize with your student athletes. You also need to keep your eyes and ears open and be a great communicator, and you definitely need to be organized. It is also essential to stay current with new programs and treatments. As athletic trainers we have to get continuing-education units to make sure that we are doing all that we can for our athletes. When we go to these workshops we learn things that we can bring back with us. Many workshops are about getting hold of a problem before it develops. The idea is to screen the athletes and assess their conditions so that they will not get hurt.

Scout the terrain. Different settings have different job requirements. Athletic trainers in hospitals and clinics generally have regular hours, while those who work with school or professional sports teams may put in longer hours based on game and travel schedules. Wherever they work, athletic trainers' main concern is to provide quality health care that enables people to prevent and recover from injuries and perform at their highest levels. Certified trainers can contact local schools and clinics and check with organizations like the National Athletic Trainers' Association for job openings in their areas.

Essential Gear

Know how to use an automated external defibrillator. This portable device, commonly known as an AED, automatically restores normal heart rhythm in cases of sudden cardiac arrest. This condition, in which the heart abruptly stops pumping blood throughout the body, is a leading cause of death among young athletes. Since prompt use of an AED can save lives, the National Athletic Trainers' Association urges AED training for all likely first responders to medical emergencies.

Find the path that's right for you. All paths start with obtaining a bachelor's degree from a school with an accredited athletic trainer program, then passing a certification test. Requirements may vary among the 365 U.S. colleges and universities that provide accredited programs. Check with individual schools about options for earning degrees. For example, if a person is a nurse or other health professional, some schools might give credit for courses already taken. Other schools may have online programs, or let career changers attend school part-time or at night. Once on the job, trainers can strive to become head trainers, or perhaps move from sports to clinical work.

Landmarks

If you are in your twenties . . . Now is the time to earn a college degree if you do not already have one. This will enable you to enroll in an accredited athletic trainer program. Those who have a degree in another field can also enroll in such a program. People who are not ready to make a long-term commitment to such schoolwork can take courses in first aid and CPR to learn valuable skills and see whether they are suited for a career in health care.

If you are in your thirties or forties . . . Becoming an athletic trainer could be a natural move for people who have worked as nurses or in allied health fields. High school teachers, particularly those who have coached or taught physical education, may likewise find work as an athletic trainer a rewarding change of careers. But wherever career changers may currently work, they will need to adjust their schedules to return to school and earn their degrees.

If you are in your fifties . . . The educational requirements and day-to-day demands of the job may be difficult to master for anyone without a background in health care. But people who have taken early retirement, have the time for schooling, and are interested in medicine could find athletic training to be an enjoyable and stimulating line of work. Hospitals or clinics could provide the best setting, since the pace of the work would be slower and more predictable than the pace of sports-related jobs.

If you are over sixty . . . Volunteer work can be an option, particularly if you have been a paramedic or know first aid. But the legal and other requirements for performing hands-on medical work are rigorous, and you will need to check first with the school or health care facility with which you are seeking employment. One possibility might be to shadow a trainer to learn about the work and any volunteer opportunities that may exist.

Further Resources

The **Board of Certification** provides detailed information about the national certification examination for athletic trainers and offers an online registration form for people taking the test.   http://www.bocatc.org

The **Commission on Accreditation of Athletic Training Education** provides a complete list of colleges and universities with accredited programs.   http://www.caate.net

The **National Athletic Trainers' Association** provides a wealth of news and information about educational requirements, health and safety recommendations, job listings, and other issues related to the field. http://www.nata.org

Fitness Worker

Fitness Worker

Career Compasses

Here is the breakdown of what it takes to be a successful fitness worker.

Relevant Knowledge of the field (25%)

Caring about the individuals and groups whom you instruct (25%)

Organizational Skills to plan and carry out exercise and training programs (25%)

Communication Skills to teach exercises and maintain enthusiasm among clients (25%)

Destination: Fitness Worker

Fitness workers offer words of encouragement in health clubs, aerobics centers, weight rooms, and other venues. These workers, also known as personal trainers and group exercise instructors, lead groups and individuals in physical activities ranging from stretching and cardiovascular training to yoga and Pilates exercises.

The demand for fitness workers is rapidly growing in today's health-conscious world. Their sources of employment have expanded from gyms and similar facilities to sites that include spas, cruise ships, commercial workplaces, and clients' homes. This furnishes fitness workers with a variety of prospective employers and the option of going into business for themselves.

Since their job focuses on health and fitness and requires physical exertion, these workers need to be in top shape themselves. They should be skilled at whatever form of exercise they are teaching, and be able to demonstrate the correct technique. They should also enjoy working with people and be outgoing, patient, and enthusiastic, and be able to teach and listen well. Above all, they must be skillful motivators in order to keep clients coming back for regular sessions of what can be hard work. Safety is also a key concern of people in this field. Personal and group sessions must be challenging enough to promote health and fitness, but not so demanding as to cause clients to overexert or injure themselves. Group instructors often set their exercise programs to music to energize their classes, and perform right along with the students. ("Gonna Fly Now," the soaring theme from the hit film "Rocky," is said to be the most popular workout accompaniment in health clubs.) Instructors keep an eye on groups of clients as they exercise in order to catch and correct mistakes.

Essential Gear

Understand the workout equipment. Fitness workers employ training equipment ranging from workout balls and balance boards to treadmills and weight machines. Pilates strength and flexibility exercises are performed on mats and a variety of specialized apparatus. Fitness workers must fully understand their gear and be able to instruct students in its safe and proper use.

While there are no specific educational requirements for fitness workers, an associate's degree or bachelor's degree can help people get jobs and advance in the field. Typical college programs may include courses in aerobics, nutrition, health education, and kinesiology—the science of human movement. Despite this lack of a specific educational program, most personal trainers still need to be certified before working with clients. Group instructors may not require a credential at first, but it can become an important tool for advancement. Most certifying groups require candidates to have a high school diploma and be able to perform cardiopulmonary resuscitation. The groups provide courses and home-study kits and conduct examinations that typically include 150 multiple-choice questions, and can require anywhere from a few weeks to more than a year of preparation. Once certified, trainers need to earn continuing education credits to qualify for recertification every two or three years. Such credits can be gained in ways that include giving presentations, attending conferences, and participating in online seminars.

Since many groups offer certificates, requirements can vary and aspiring workers should deal with respected and well-known organizations. The National Commission for Certifying Agencies, a nonprofit group, accredits certifying organizations that apply to it and meet its standards. Specialized groups may have their own certification requirements. For example, the Pilates Method Alliance awards its certificate to instructors who complete at least 450 hours of comprehensive Pilates teacher training. The Yoga Alliance registers instructors who have received at least 200 hours of teacher training. Many fitness workers decide to enter the field after taking a class or course of personal instruction themselves.

Essential Gear

Know computers and personal digital assistants. Web sites, e-mail, and software programs can be as crucial as exercise equipment to success in this field. Fitness workers maintain and build their client lists, keep workout schedules, chart group and individual progress reports, and record billing statements—all of which can be simplified by using computer programs. Online social networks can be particularly valuable marketing tools for personal trainers who run their own businesses.

For such individuals, the experience of being in good physical condition creates a desire to help others get in shape too.

Opportunities are highly varied in this field. Some people may begin as personal trainers who focus on weights and traditional exercise, and then specialize in yoga or Pilates. Other specialized areas include instructing older clients and people with illnesses or injuries—dimensions that require additional training and allow fitness workers to broaden their practices. A key choice for workers is whether to join the staff of a health club or other location or start their own businesses. Those working in clubs can advance to positions such as head trainer or fitness director—jobs calling for management skills that can be gained by enrolling in college courses or continuing education programs. Similar skills are useful for workers who become self-employed. Many people begin their careers in health clubs and then venture into business for themselves, working out of their homes or opening studios. Those who choose this route must be able to market their services in a fast-growing and increasingly competitive field.

Fitness jobs are projected to grow much faster than average in coming years, thanks in part to the explosive growth of interest in Pilates and yoga. The U.S. Bureau of Labor Statistics says the category "Fitness trainers and aerobics instructors" will expand from 235,000 jobs in 2006 to 298,000 in 2016. Median annual pay for the category was $29,210 in 2008, with the bottom 10 percent earning up to $16,120 and the top 10 percent making more than $60,760.

You Are Here

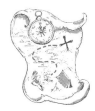

Determine your interest and ability to become a fitness worker.

Have you taken an exercise class or worked with a personal trainer? This can be the first step to entering the field since it demonstrates an interest in health and fitness. Many instructors start out as students, although it is not required to do so. But getting into shape by taking a group or individual class can be a good introduction to the duties, qualities, and skills of experienced fitness workers.

Are you enthusiastic about working with people? As with many sports jobs, a desire to help others is crucial for success in this field. Fitness workers are teachers who derive satisfaction from the physical gains their clients make. Such gains have mental and emotional components as well, since being in good shape can increase a person's confidence and sense of well-being.

Do subjects like human anatomy and the science of human movement interest you? Such knowledge is at the core of a fitness worker's job. Successful trainers and group instructors know how exercise, weight training, and related activities affect the body, and how to prescribe and supervise them in beneficial ways. Trainers also understand the role of individual differences between trainees and how these differences can influence the prevention of injuries. Developing these capabilities to a high degree can take years of experience and learning.

Navigating the Terrain

I want to become a fitness worker

Take a class or visit clubs and talk with instructors to learn about the job

Enroll in a national certification program

Apply for position in a health club, gym, or other facility

Become a fitness worker

Organizing Your Expedition

Before you set out, know where you are going.

Decide on a destination. Since this field is rich in possibilities, picking a long-term goal can be a helpful first move. Do you want to go into business for yourself or to work in a health-and-fitness facility with an opportunity to advance to a managerial post? Fitness work has specialties within specialties as well. A Pilates instructor may focus on athletes or musicians, for example, or teach people how to become instructors themselves. Job situations can also be fluid. For example, a fitness worker might go from a health club to self-employment, and then back to a club as an independent contractor.

Scout the terrain. The Web offers a wealth of information about becoming a fitness worker and getting certified. In fact, so many sites hawk certification programs that you will probably need help sorting them out. Learn which ones have been accredited. Speak with certified workers

Notes from the Field

Chris Kandianis
Self-employed personal trainer specializing in Pilates
Westford, Massachusetts

What were you doing before you decided to change careers?

I was marketing director for a software company, generating leads, managing relationships with resellers, and basically coming up with a marketing program to increase sales.

Why did you change your career?

I had a desire to do something more fulfilling and rewarding personally. I have always had a passion for fitness. I have been a runner and done swimming and biking and rock climbing and had taken lots of Pilates classes. I gravitated toward Pilates because it had a strong physical component and helped people with physical conditions.

How did you make the transition?

I started by taking courses and doing some teaching. I bought some equipment and taught at a studio briefly. I have certifications from the American Council of Sports Medicine as a personal trainer and from STOTT Pilates for Pilates. The STOTT program took a year and a half to complete and required a written and practical exam.

What are the keys to success in your new career?

I have a passion for what I am doing—providing people with a valuable service and helping them to derive benefits from the service. Some of it is certainly managing the business side—marketing, finding new people to come to classes, and retaining people. Being really competent in the subject matter is important as well. I continue to go to training to upgrade my skills, and every single class I go to I come away with something new. Networking with other health professionals is important too.

about the programs they completed. Some programs may have more rigorous requirements than others and better prepare you for a successful career. If you do not have an associate's or a bachelor's degree, this can be the time to explore college physical education and related programs.

Find the path that's right for you. Armed with the information that you have acquired, sign up for a certification program, network with experienced workers to learn about job openings, and take an exercise or other type of fitness class if you have not already done so. Be open to various activities and experiences: you may find an activity that you have not previously explored strongly appeals to you.

Landmarks

If you are in your twenties . . . If you are a fitness buff, stepping into this line of work may be a natural move. Certification programs are available through home study, which allows you to learn the field and get credentialed while working at your current job. At the same time, you can explore openings in the field and be prepared to take a position once you become certified.

If you are in your thirties or forties . . . Similar opportunities are available to you as those in their twenties. Moreover, if you have a background in business or marketing, the experience can be helpful, particularly if you are interested in becoming self-employed. Fitness work is an occupation that has plenty of room for skills developed in a previous career, such as oral communication, math and statistics, and anatomy and physiology.

If you are in your fifties . . . Part-time work in a health club, or self-employment that lets you set your own hours, could be for you. Full-time trainers often see one client after another with little chance to rest in between; you may not want to work that hard. People with a background in health care may find their knowledge particularly useful in dealing with clients on a one-to-one basis.

If you are over sixty . . . Individuals who have retired from another occupation can still enter this field, and those with an interest in Pilates or yoga have been known to do so. Your life experience is an asset as you work with a rapidly expanding senior population, who are more inclined to trust those of their age group.

Further Resources

The **American College of Sports Medicine**, **American Council on Exercise**, and the **National Academy of Sports Medicine** are among the organizations that offer certification programs for fitness workers. http://www.acsm.org, http://www.acefitness.org, and http://www.nacsm.org

IDEA Health and Fitness Association provides research and educational materials for people in the health and fitness field. http://www.ideafit.com

The **National Council of Certifying Agencies** accredits certifying groups that apply and meet its standards. http://www.noca.org/NCCA-Accreditation/NCCAMissionandVision/tabid/90/Default.as

Athletic Director

Athletic Director

Career Compasses

Here is the breakdown of what it takes to become an athletic director.

Relevant Knowledge of how to carry out the job's responsibilities (40%)

Caring about the success of the athletic program (20%)

Organizational Skills to conduct a wide range of duties (20%)

Communication Skills to deal with players, coaches, alumni, and other constituencies (20%)

Destination: Athletic Director

Athletic directors are the chief executive officers of academic sports programs. They oversee operations ranging from high school sports offices to university athletic departments with hundreds of employees and annual budgets that can top $50 million. Since sports teams are often the public face of a college or university and a source of pride and revenue, the athletic director's job can be quite a high-profile and demanding one.

Athletic directors have many duties in common wherever they work. They determine budgets, evaluate coaches, supervise staffs, and organize schedules, among other responsibilities. They deal with student athletes, parents, fans, and alumni, and represent their departments in meetings with other administrators and before the general public. They work long hours and frequently put in six-day weeks, since many sporting events take place on the weekend. The job calls for a love of sports, strong communication and administrative skills, and the ability to multitask. Many athletic directors have played or coached a sport, which helps them relate to the student athletes whose programs they supervise. Athletics are part of a school's educational experience, and directors should seek to ensure that they are seen in that light.

Essential Gear

The influence of Title IX. No law has had a greater impact on athletic programs in recent years than Title IX of the Education Amendments of 1972. The measure bars sexual discrimination in high school and college sports. Male and female teams must receive equivalent funding, for example, and athletic scholarships must be equally available to both sexes in colleges and universities. Athletic directors must bring their programs and budgets into compliance with this sweeping measure and educate coaches, athletes, alumni, and others about its impact; violation of the law can result in a loss of federal funds.

At colleges and universities, athletic directors hire coaches and are deeply involved in raising funds to support sports programs and facilities. This includes raising money for staff salaries and athletic scholarships, and for financing stadium improvements that can cost tens of millions of dollars. To secure funds, athletic directors arrange sponsorships, negotiate broadcast rights to football and basketball games, and tap alumni and other contributors. Marketing, advertising, and ticket sales all fall under the athletic director's purview as well.

Recruiting athletes is another task that distinguishes college and university directors from those at the high school level. Small colleges typically recruit players from nearby regions; major universities scout and draw athletes from throughout the country. While coaches are normally in charge of these efforts, they consult with athletic directors on matters such as travel and recruiting budgets.

As directors go about their jobs, they must pay close attention to compliance matters. Schools, conferences, and organizations like the National Collegiate Athletic Association enforce regulations covering everything from recruiting requirements to gender issues. Violation of the rules can cause schools to be sanctioned and endanger an athletic director's career; news of such infractions quickly turns into headlines.

Essential Gear

Become familiar with NCAA bylaws. The association's thick manuals lay down the rules that athletic directors must follow. Each of the three college divisions has hundreds of pages of bylaws covering everything from the definition of an amateur athlete to the number of meals that schools can provide to players they are recruiting. Sample Division I rule: "Receipt by a student-athlete of an award, benefit or expense allowance not authorized by NCAA legislation renders the student-athlete ineligible for athletic competition in the sport for which the improper award, benefit or expense was received." The bylaws are both exhaustive and regularly updated, so athletic directors must keep up with the changes.

Regulations can vary from one university division to another and even within a division. For example, some conferences that play in Division I of the NCAA— the highest level—are required to offer athletic scholarships, while other conferences in the division can choose to award them or not. Division II conferences have the option of providing such scholarships, but schools in Division III cannot hand out such aid.

The role of athletic directors can vary from division to division. In major universities with dozens of sports teams and large athletic departments, directors may concentrate on tasks like fund-raising, and delegate some duties to staffs of assistants. Directors at smaller schools may have a single assistant and spend more time on day-to-day activities and with student athletes. "You are a jack of all trades," says Jason Fein, athletic director at Drew University, a Division III school in Madison, New Jersey.

Jobs for education administrators are expected to grow about as fast as the average for all occupations, according to the U.S. Bureau of Labor Statistics, which includes athletic directors in this category. The department says the median annual wage for administrators was $71,630 in 2008, with the top 10 percent earning more than $124,600, and the bottom 10 percent making less than $38,900. However, some athletic directors at large universities that are traditional sports powers may earn salaries that approach $1 million.

Schools set their own qualifications for the job of athletic director. A bachelor's degree is typically the minimum educational requirement;

many colleges and universities want master's degrees as well. Preferred courses of study include sports marketing, administration, and facilities management. Advancement in the field calls for networking and working through the ranks. High school athletic directors have often been teachers and coaches, and some may move to college positions. Colleges and universities have numerous athletic jobs that can provide valuable experience. These include public relations, marketing, and raising funds for sports programs. Individuals in such jobs can make contacts and win promotions. Once at the college level, athletic directors may also move among the different NCAA divisions. An assistant athletic director at a Division I university might become the head director at a Division II or Division III school. Conversely, the athletic director at a small university could join a Division I school as an assistant and have a chance at the top position.

You Are Here

Determine your interest and ability to be an athletic director.

Do you love sports? This is the core quality needed for the job. Athletic directors work long days and weeks and are under constant pressure to produce winning programs that comply with a vast number of rules. Fundraising can be a huge responsibility at the college level. A dedication to sports, and a commitment to working both with and on behalf of young athletes, are essential qualities for anyone considering a career in this field.

How organized are you? Athletic directors must be highly organized to handle the wide range of duties they are called on to perform. Versatility is crucial as well, since directors need to be as comfortable with financial and budgetary issues as they are with negotiating sponsorships and evaluating coaches and athletes. While the athletic directors of Division I universities may have large staffs to help them carry out their functions, the director is ultimately responsible for the final results.

Are you good at public relations? The athletic director's job is a highly public one, especially at the college and university level. Directors give speeches and hold news conferences, and meet with alumni and booster

Navigating the Terrain

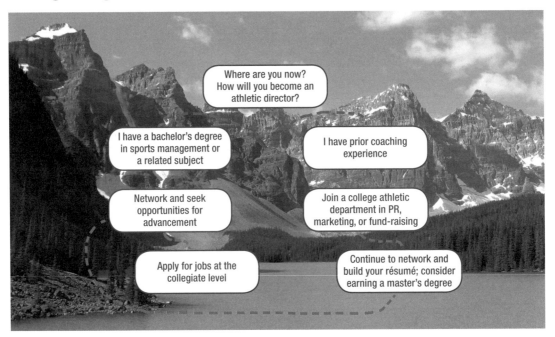

groups to encourage financial contributions and maintain fan support. Directors must be skilled at dealing with people when supervising their staffs and dividing up resources among the dozens of teams that colleges and universities field.

Organizing Your Expedition

Before you set out, know where you are going.

Decide on a destination. Do you want to work in a high school or a small college or large university? Keep in mind that the job is likely to become increasingly pressure-filled the larger the school. The athletic director of a major university with a nationwide base of alumni and fans stands to win wide acclaim when the teams are successful, but risks being ousted when they are not. The same risks apply at smaller colleges, of course, but the emphasis on winning can be less intense. Athletic directors tend to be more specialized at larger schools since the presence of large staffs lets them focus on tasks like fund-raising. Wherever athletic directors work, the job calls for willingness to put in long hours and the ability to do many things at once.

Scout the terrain. For high school teachers who aspire to be athletic directors, coaching is a natural first step. Interested teachers can keep an eye out for coaching or athletic director opportunities in their own schools or others in the area. For people who want to be athletic directors in college, *The Chronicle of Higher Education* and the NCAA post job listings from around the country on their Web sites. The National Association of Collegiate Directors of Athletics lists jobs and offers internships as well. Get to know what it means to be an athletic director by visiting college athletics departments and talking with directors, assistants, and other people who work there.

Find the path that's right for you. Networking is key ingredient for success in this line of work. Newcomers may start out in athletic-department marketing or public relations jobs to gain experience and make contacts. Joining the National Association of Collegiate Directors of Athletics is a useful way to meet people and learn about jobs and developments in the field. Earning a master's degree can boost your chances for advancement. The top jobs in major programs are extremely competitive, which puts a premium on building a reputation for sound judgment, and developing a wide range of administrative and related skills.

Landmarks

If you are in your twenties . . . There are many opportunities for people to work in college athletic departments, particularly if they have a bachelor's degree in a sports-related field. Large universities have numerous entry-level positions, including graduate assistant programs that can become launching pads for careers leading to an athletic director's job. This can also be the time to enroll in a master's degree program, which many universities offer online. Job opportunities are more limited in high schools, where staffs are smaller, but if you are a teacher or a coach you already have a place to start.

If you are in your thirties or forties . . . Career changers who have played or coached a sport may find this the time right to move into an

Notes from the Field
Tim Pernetti
Director—intercollegiate athletics, Rutgers University
New Brunswick, New Jersey

What were you doing before you decided to change careers?

I spent 15 years in the television and media business beginning at ABC sports in programming, and most recently I served as executive vice president at the CBS College Sports Network, formerly CSTV: College Sports Television. In 2003 I left ABC-TV and the mainstream network business to create the programming and content strategy at CSTV, then a startup, and to bring relationships that I had developed in college sports to the network. In six years we built a network that was devoted exclusively to college sports, was purchased by CBS TV for $325 million in 2006 and is now distributed nationally in 32 million households.

Why did you change your career?

I never thought about becoming a director of athletics at a university. Having said that, I always stayed close to Rutgers, my alma mater, and have witnessed the peaks and valleys that the athletic department has lived through. When the call came about the Rutgers opportunity, it

athletic-department career. Alumni who have played on a college team may leverage that experience to obtain a position at their old school, or even move straight into the athletic director's office. People in fields such as finance, marketing, or public relations may discover that athletic departments welcome their skills with jobs and opportunities for advancement.

If you are in your fifties . . . Your opportunities may be similar to those available to people in their thirties and forties if you have the necessary skills, although the chances of advancing to the position of athletic director will be probably be less. Seasoned administrators who change their careers may find assistant directorships available at large universities.

If you are over sixty . . . Athletic departments can still make use of your skills, but do not expect to become the director. At the same time, volun-

appealed to my passion for my alma mater and interest in its success, and also applied to my experience in collegiate athletics from a media perspective. I feel fortunate to have been part of a startup network that paved the way for so many collegiate sports networks (ESPNU, The Mtn, Big Ten Network, etc), and it was appealing to me to experience collegiate athletics from the on-campus perspective. I've always believed in chasing my passion, not just looking for a job, and Rutgers is the perfect dish to serve my passion.

How did you make the transition?

The transition is ongoing, but I made a commitment the moment I accepted the job, which was to be accessible to everyone inside and outside the university community. As an athletics director, there are many constituents that you interact with on a daily basis. Being accessible helps to bring athletics and the university closer together. Making a successful transition is all about being accessible and developing relationships.

What are the keys to success in your new career?

The keys to success in this job, or any leadership position like it, are to cultivate and develop relationships, to set and effectively communicate a vision, and the ability to make the tough decisions.

teer opportunities may exist inside the office and on the field. On game days, for example, a person familiar with statistics could work with the crews that chart plays and keep track of statistics as contests unfold.

Further Resources

The Chronicle of Higher Education lists job opportunities in athletic departments throughout the country.   http://www.chronicle.com

The **National Association of Collegiate Directors of Athletics** provides information on jobs, internships, and educational opportunities. http://www.nacda.com

The **National Collegiate Athletic Association** provides job listings and the full text of college division bylaws online.   http://www.ncaa.org

The **National Federation of State High School Associations** provides information about high school athletic programs.   http://www.nfhs.org

Sports Agent

Sports Agent

Career Compasses

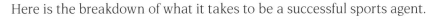

Here is the breakdown of what it takes to be a successful sports agent.

Relevant Knowledge of sports and sports contracts and the rules that govern agent conduct (40%)

Communication Skills to negotiate effectively on your clients' behalf (25%)

Organizational Skills to develop programs to maximize your clients' earnings (25%)

Caring about your clients' needs (10%)

Destination: Sports Agent

Agents are the dealmakers of professional sports. They bargain for salaries and fees on behalf of players, and provide services ranging from securing endorsements to offering legal and financial advice. Their clients are members of professional teams and individual athletes in sports such as tennis and golf, and can include coaches and team executives.

The role of the sports agent is relatively new. Agents first came to prominence in the 1970s with the advent of free agency—the ability of players to market their services freely to teams once their contracts expired. Courts made this possible by striking down clauses that had tied athletes to the clubs that first signed them. At the same time, competition for players from new sources like the American Football League—now part of the National Football League—sparked bidding wars. These developments, together with the growing use of sports stars to endorse products and services, drove player incomes skyward, and led athletes to hire agents to represent them. With seven-figure salaries now the rule in big-time team sports—major league baseball teams pay their players nearly $3 million a year on average—the job of sports agent can provide high financial rewards. Agents typically work for commissions that range from 3 percent to 5 percent of a player's salary. In addition, they pocket a share of any bonuses they negotiate for their clients, and take a cut of endorsement deals. Not every agent works this way: Some may charge flat fees or hourly rates in lieu of commissions.

Essential Gear

Use cell phones and personal digital assistants. Sports agents must be available day and night to clients, team executives, corporate marketing managers, and others. Clients tend to regard agents as all-around advisers and may them call at any time with questions about financial or personal matters. Being constantly available strengthens bonds with clients and helps to maintain their confidence in an agent's services. Agents keep in close touch with teams and sponsors during contract negotiations, and stand ready to seize opportunities as they arise.

Agents must be passionate about sports and shrewd bargainers on behalf of their clients. Like all good negotiators, agents need a strong sense of timing and must know when to cut a deal and when to push for better terms. Agents who win smart deals for their clients may represent them throughout their playing careers, and continue to provide advice when athletes' playing days are over.

The first task of agents is to locate clients. "It is a matter of networking," says Gary Glick, an attorney and CEO of Synergy Sports Inc. in Dallas, Texas, which represents NFL players. After getting to know some stars on the Dallas Cowboys, Glick got his start as an agent by negotiating for them. His company now receives referrals from scouts and other contacts that spot college athletes with the talent to succeed at the professional level.

Becoming an agent can be a natural move for attorneys, because they are already quite familiar with contracts. Accountants and financial advisers who work with sports clients may also choose to put on an agent's hat. Newcomers to the field can prospect for clients by attending games and getting to know players, coaches, and scouts. Some agents have begun their careers by representing players they knew in college. Others have taken internships with major agencies like IMG World and gone to work for those companies. Mark Steinberg, who represents golf great Tiger Woods, began as an intern at IMG and went on to head its golf division.

The business of signing up clients is fiercely competitive. In their rush to represent college stars that can become top draft choices and command high salaries, some agents have been caught violating recruiting rules by offering players incentives such as cash or cars to sign with them. The 1996 hit film *Jerry Maguire*, with a ruthless sports agent among its characters, also has colored perceptions of the job.

Before agents can bargain on behalf of a player in any of the four major league team sports—baseball, basketball, football, and hockey—they must be certified by that league's players union. Requirements vary among the unions. Agents for members of the National Football League Players Association must have a degree in law or another post-graduate subject, and pass a 60-question multiple-choice test. The major league baseball players union has no educational or test requirement, but agents must have a client on a 40-man big league roster in order to be certified. Once cleared by the unions, sports agents can be self-employed or work for firms such as SFX Sports and Octagon,

Essential Gear

Maintain personal contacts. The agent's job is a social one that calls for building up contacts among players, teams, and sponsors. Agents constantly network to find clients, and cultivate contacts with team and league officials to follow events throughout the sports world. Agents also work to befriend managers in companies that manufacture endorsable products. The agent for a golf star is apt to spend time getting to know brand managers for golfing equipment, for example.

in addition to many smaller ones. Besides representing athletes, such firms provide a range of services that may include managing entertainers and promoting fashion shows and other events.

Job prospects for sports agents are projected to grow faster than average. The U.S. Bureau of Labor Statistics says positions for agents in the "performing arts, spectator sports, and related industries" will expand from nearly 8,500 jobs in 2006 to nearly 9,700 in 2016, for a gain of 14 percent. The median wage for such agents was $62,940 in 2008, with the bottom 10 percent earning up to $27,810, and the top 10 percent making as much or more than $166,400 a year. But that figure merely hints at the earnings of some agents, since those who represent top athletes can pocket seven-figure incomes.

You Are Here

Determine your interest and ability to become a sports agent.

How passionate about sports are you? A dedication to sports and the athletes who play them is essential to a career as a sports agent. Without a deep knowledge of sports and what it takes for athletes to succeed, agents cannot evaluate their clients' skills and earnings potential, or put the athlete's best foot forward in contract talks. Some agents have been athletes themselves, but this is not a requirement.

How versatile are you? Sports agents are negotiators, promoters, and advisers all rolled into one. While the core of their jobs is bargaining on behalf of athletes, they also must market themselves to prospective clients and promote their clients' interests to teams and corporate sponsors. These roles can require persistence bordering on brashness, and strong communication skills—qualities that help agents win the trust of their clients, and the acquiescence of those on the other side of deals.

How comfortable with contracts are you? Contracts are the language that athletes' careers are written in, and agents must be familiar with a wide range of documents and their terms. In addition to negotiating deals between players and teams and corporate sponsors, agents must take labor agreements between leagues and unions for players into account. Agents must comply with university and NCAA rules when dealing with college athletes, and need to keep track of changes in the rules.

Navigating the Terrain

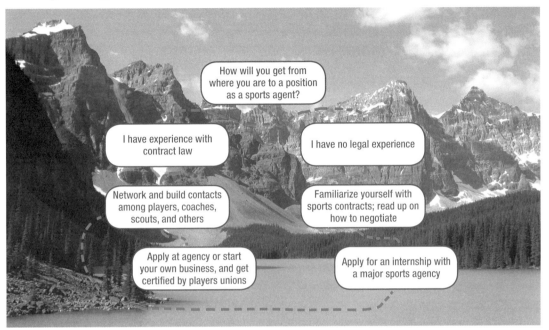

How will you get from where you are to a position as a sports agent?

I have experience with contract law

I have no legal experience

Network and build contacts among players, coaches, scouts, and others

Familiarize yourself with sports contracts; read up on how to negotiate

Apply at agency or start your own business, and get certified by players unions

Apply for an internship with a major sports agency

Organizing Your Expedition

Before you set out, know where you are going.

Decide on a destination. This occupation can be tough to break into. While college internships may provide an entry into agencies, the competition for such positions is normally keen. On the other hand, going into business for yourself can be difficult without first knowing prospective clients. But becoming a sports agent is obviously not impossible. Anyone with a passion for sports can network with athletes and others in the industry to establish contacts and seek opportunities.

Scout the terrain. Some agencies represent athletes in a single sport, while others are not specialized. If you are an attorney or financial adviser, you may already have players or coaches among your clients who can point to athletes who may need agents. If you have a friend who is a good athlete, that may be the place to start. In 2005, basketball super-

Stories from the Field

Bob Woolf
Pioneering sports agent
Boston, Massachusetts

The man considered a founder of the sports agent business began his career as a lawyer. The late Bob Woolf was an attorney in Boston in 1964 when a Red Sox player whom he advised about taxes sought his help in handling endorsement requests. Other players soon learned of Woolf's bargaining prowess, and he went on to serve as agent to some of the top athletes in professional sports. "I get credit for being brilliant for having had the foresight to stake out this new frontier," Woolf wrote in his 1990 book *Friendly Persuasion*, "but the truth is that I just happened to be in the right place at the right time."

Woolf brought skills honed as a lawyer and litigator to the task of negotiating contracts for players. "You do not have to be disagreeable to disagree," was one of his mottos. "I never think of negotiating against anyone," he wrote, "I work with people to come to an agreement."

Like a lawyer preparing his case, Woolf stressed the importance of research before contract talks. This included assessing a player's market value and knowing the needs and personalities of those on the opposite side of the table. Woolf kept the word "demand" out of his vocabulary, using terms like "suggestion" and "recommendation" instead. "If someone marched into my office with their list of demands, I'd want to show them out," he said.

For all his civility, Woolf was happy to make full use of any leverage that he had. After San Francisco '49ers quarterback Joe Montana won his fourth Super Bowl title, sponsors clamored for him to endorse their wares. "I made sure that I took advantage of the overwhelming leverage," Woolf boasted, "and negotiated long-term, guaranteed contracts at the highest range of fair-market value for Joe's services."

Woolf thought some attorneys had habits that jeopardized deals. Among them was a tendency to harp on things that could go wrong. But good negotiators keep "looking for the best ways to keep the process moving," he wrote, instead of forever finding "gray clouds in silver linings." For lawyer-turned-sports-agent Woolf, a mutually satisfactory agreement was always the bottom line.

star LeBron James, one of the most valuable properties in all sports, fired his agent and hired three friends from high school to represent him.

Find the path that's right for you. Your path will start with the people you meet through internships or by networking on your own. Such contacts will play a key role in helping you reach your goal. If a particular sport interests you, you may decide to represent athletes in that field. The growth of professional leagues in sports such as volleyball and track and field widens the range of players who may be available.

Landmarks

If you are in your twenties . . . An internship could be the gateway to a career as a sports agent if you are in college or graduate school. Look around to see which agencies offer internships and tailor your application to meet their needs. Large firms often post internship opportunities on their Web sites. Such positions are typically unpaid and available to students who receive academic credit for them. If you are out of school or unable to get an internship, this is a good time to start networking.

If you are in your thirties or forties . . . Lawyers, accountants, and marketing managers all possess skills that are useful in the sports agent field. People who fit this description may know prospective clients or have contacts at agencies that are looking for agents or different kinds of expertise. If you do not know any athletes you can seek out those who do, including coaches, trainers, sportswriters, and others who are part of the sports world.

If you are in your fifties . . . Connections with the sports industry are particularly vital at this point: Indeed, knowing a promising athlete could make you a good candidate for an agency to hire. Continue to network and cultivate personal relationships by attending games, particularly lower-level leagues where access to players is more open than in the pros. Contact the human relations departments at agencies to learn about what it takes to work there.

If you are over sixty . . . Your skills and contacts can remain useful to agencies, particularly small ones that need part-time help. You can also seek volunteer opportunities: Agencies that hire unpaid interns may be happy to draw on your know-how as well. Even if you do not work directly with athletes, you will be in a workplace that does, and that can be a stimulating environment for anyone who loves sports.

Further Resources

IMG World lists job openings and posts information about internships on its Web site. http://www.imgworld.com

Octagon lists job and internship openings on its Web site. http://www.octagonna.com

Sports Equipment Manager

Sports Equipment Manager

Career Compasses

Here is the breakdown of what it takes to become an athletic equipment manager.

Relevant Knowledge of equipment (30%)

Organizational Skills to order, inventory, and maintain equipment (25%)

Communication Skills to deal with coaches, players, trainers, and others (25%)

Caring about the comfort and safety of athletes (20%)

Destination: Sports Equipment Manager

Before they can take the court or field, athletes must don the proper uniforms and gear. Providing them is the job of the sports equipment manager, a vital behind-the-scenes member of the sports world. In addition to outfitting players with game-day uniforms, equipment managers are responsible for practice apparel and everything from baseball bats and hockey sticks to shot puts and pole vault poles. In a word, these managers order and maintain the clothing and equipment that make practice and competition possible.

The duties of a sports equipment manager can vary in scope from high school to college to the professional level. Wherever they work, equipment managers must be highly organized and detail-oriented to keep track of the numerous items that sports teams use. A major college football team may have 100 players, for example, and each needs a complete set of properly fitted uniforms, helmets, pads, shoes, and practice clothing. A typical team may have three sets of shoes to be used on different kinds of fields. Andy Dixon, head equipment manager at the University of Illinois in Champaign-Urbana, says a single football player can go through 10 practice T-shirts a year as a result of constant wear and washing. Managers also outfit coaches with apparel, including game-day slacks, jackets and polo shirts.

The manager's job starts with ordering equipment and may include budgeting as well. "Managers are more responsible for their budgets today because school administrators know they can depend on them," says Jon Falk, head equipment manager at the University of Michigan and executive director of the Athletic Equipment Managers Association. Founded in 1974, the AEMA certifies managers and works to upgrade their skills. Ordering gear calls for a thorough knowledge of the equipment and an ability to anticipate players' needs. While returning athletes have already been measured, new ones also must be taken into account. At the University of Illinois, Dixon orders football uniforms one year in advance without knowing what sizes new players will take. "We have to guesstimate," he says.

Essential Gear

The need for helmet-fitting tools. Modern helmets are complex protective devices that must be fit properly for maximum comfort and safety. Football helmets consist of a hard plastic shell and adjustable padding that incorporates air bladders to customize the fit. Facemasks must be fitted as well. Equipment managers use calipers to measure a player's head size, and inflation bulbs to pump in the correct amount of air. Screwdrivers, wrenches, and pliers are part of the tool kit when it comes to fitting and adjusting facemasks and chinstraps.

Once it arrives, all equipment is carefully inventoried and fitted. Protective headgear must comply with safety guidelines set by the National Operating Committee on Standards for Athletic Equipment. Helmets for football, baseball, hockey, polo, and lacrosse are all covered by the rules. "When we get a new helmet we log it in and track it," says Mike Royster, head equipment manager at the University of Tennessee in Chattanooga and president of the AEMA. "Every time it is reconditioned we make a note of it. Equipment managers have been told that they better be able to take care of these helmets and have the records to show for it."

Besides being organized, equipment managers need good communication skills. "Managers deal with head coaches and assistants, and players, trainers, and sports information people," says Royster. Managers must be good listeners, particularly when a new head coach arrives with his or her own methods of getting things done.

Working hours have grown longer along with team training and practice schedules. This translates into constant tasks for the equipment room. At the University of Illinois, Dixon says his department may launder nearly 1,000 pounds of football gear and towels a day, even in summer when no games are scheduled. And while most departments send torn clothing out to be repaired, his staff does sewing jobs in-house.

Essential Gear

Brush up on your computer skills. With the advent of centralized equipment purchasing, managers need to be familiar with basic programs like Microsoft Excel. All orders for teams at multi-campus state universities typically go through a central computer system, for example, requiring managers to enter the data and track the progress of purchasing requests.

As the role of the equipment manager has become more professional, the requirements for getting hired have increased as well. Many employers now want job candidates to have a bachelor's degree, and certification by the AEMA can be essential for advancement in the field. To qualify for a credential, candidates must be at least 21 and pass a test on topics that include purchasing, fitting, maintaining, and repairing uniforms and gear. Individuals must also meet one of the following combinations of requirements: a high school diploma or its equivalent, plus five years of paid work in athletic equipment management; a bachelor's degree plus two years of such employment; or a bachelor's degree plus 1,800 hours of work as a student equipment manager.

The demand for athletic equipment managers can be expected to grow steadily, thanks in part to the growth of women's sports. (The U.S. Bureau of Labor Statistics does not track athletic equipment management jobs.) As for pay, people in the athletic equipment field say annual salaries may range from about $22,000 for entry-level jobs to $100,000 for experienced head equipment managers at major universities.

You Are Here

Determine your interest and ability to be an athletic equipment manager.

Are you highly organized? Equipment managers may oversee thousands of pieces of gear and apparel for hundreds of athletes, each of whom must be fitted properly. Ordering and maintaining this equipment in good condition requires managers to keep track of a great many things at once. If attending to details drives you crazy, this is not the job for you.

Can you work long hours? With so many details to handle, equipment managers often arrive on the job before players and coaches, and remain after they have left. This calls for patience, dedication, and a desire to see the teams that you outfit succeed. It also requires a degree of self-effacement, since unlike players and coaches, equipment managers work strictly behind the scenes.

Navigating the Terrain

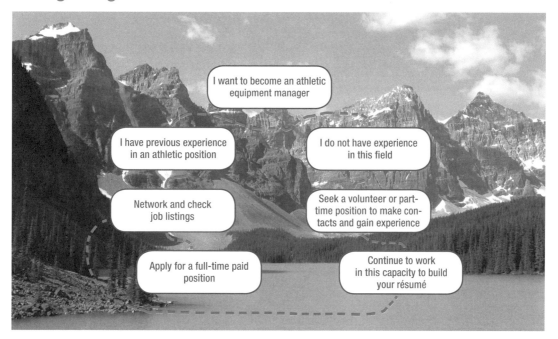

I want to become an athletic equipment manager

I have previous experience in an athletic position

I do not have experience in this field

Network and check job listings

Seek a volunteer or part-time position to make contacts and gain experience

Apply for a full-time paid position

Continue to work in this capacity to build your résumé

Notes from the Field

Andy Dixon
Head athletic equipment manager, University of Illinois
Champaign-Urbana, Illinois

What were you doing before you changed careers?

I taught health and physical education to high school students and coached football and basketball.

Why did you change your career?

I had gone to college at the University of Wyoming, where I was a running back on the football team, and had taught away from home. I wanted to get out of teaching and come back to my hometown. I saw an advertisement for an assistant equipment manager and interviewed for the job.

How did you make the transition?

It was difficult at first. As a football player in college I had been on the other side. During two-a-day practices, when the first practice was over I would go home and get something to eat and then come back. Here in the equipment room you can work from six in the morning to midnight. We are doing laundry, checking in equipment, and repairing it. My boss had been here 39 years before he retired and he helped me tremendously.

What are the keys to success in your new field?

Patience, understanding, organization, and wanting to help the athletes and the coaching staff succeed to the best of their ability on the field. A lot of times some of the best players would have troubles and people would confide in me. Players who were here 25 years ago come back to see us. They say it is amazing how some of the work principles they learned here have helped them throughout their careers.

Do you love sports? This is an essential ingredient of the job and no small part of the satisfaction that it brings. Many equipment managers have played sports or been around them since high school or college, and enjoy working with coaches and athletes and being an indispensable part of the team. This helps to explain why some managers stay on the job for decades despite its heavy time demands.

Organizing Your Expedition

Before you set out, know where you are going.

Decide on a destination. Equipment management utilizes skills found both in and out of the sports world. Purchasing agents could become equipment managers, for example, as could sporting goods representatives or persons with experience in apparel stores. If your goal is to become an equipment manager, assess the skills you possess to see which would make the best fit.

Scout the terrain. Now that you know what skills to market, check out the opportunities. You can begin making contacts with local high school, college, or professional teams to ascertain their needs. Networking with equipment managers will give you a sense of what the job may entail. You can broaden your inquiries by contacting the Athletic Equipment Managers Association to discuss your interest and get professional advice.

Find the path that's right for you. When seeking a job, emphasize your relevant skills. Remember that the position of head equipment manager generally requires years of experience, so unless you have a strong background in sports administration you will probably need to start as an assistant and work your way up. That will give you the chance to try the job of equipment manager on for size, so to speak, to see if it is right for you.

Landmarks

If you are in your twenties . . . People with a degree in sports administration can go directly into the equipment management field. Those who have the work experience required by the AEMA can take a test to earn a certificate that can advance their careers. For persons without the required experience, this can be the time to assess skills and tailor résumés to stress abilities that are useful in equipment management.

If you are in your thirties or forties . . . You probably have broadened and deepened skills that can be transferred to the equipment room. Experiences as varied as tailoring and department store buying can play a role in this job. You will want to network and make numerous contacts among people in sports to explore job possibilities. You might also consider volunteer or part-time work to help get started. Since equipment managers typically work demanding hours, they will appreciate the help.

If you are in your fifties . . . Many of the same guidelines for those in their thirties and forties apply to you. From the perspective of an employer, the increased experience you have gained at this stage of your career could make you all the more valuable. You may find that players and coaches seek you out as a seasoned, impartial, listening ear—another unofficial role of the equipment manager.

If you are over sixty . . . The volunteer opportunities are numerous, since equipment rooms operate day and night and workers have countless tasks to perform. Volunteer work could establish you as a person to be trusted and lead to a part-time or full-time job.

Further Resources

The Athletic Equipment Managers Association certifies managers, sponsors committees on continuing education and other topics of interest, and holds an annual convention.   http://www.aema1.com
The **National Operating Committee on Standards for Athletic Equipment** sets standards for sports helmets and soccer shin guards, and sponsors research on brain and spinal injuries and protective gear. http://www.nocsae.org

Sports Facility Manager

Sports Facility Manager

Career Compasses

Here is the breakdown of what it takes to be a successful sports facility manager.

Relevant Knowledge of the facilities you oversee (40%)

Organizational Skills to manage a wide range of projects, including preparation for games and events (30%)

Communication Skills to supervise workers and confer with fellow administrators (20%)

Caring about keeping facilities in top condition (10%)

Destination: Sports Facility Manager

Without managers to oversee stadiums, arenas, and other venues, sports could not be played. Managers are responsible for operating and maintaining all aspects of athletic facilities, from practice fields and press boxes to locker rooms and luxury suites. The job includes preparing facilities for games and events and organizing the personnel to staff them. Managers instruct ushers, ticket takers, box office attendants, and others about their duties, and patrol the facilities on game days to see that things runs smoothly.

Sports facilities may range from sites for high school and college sports to homes for professional teams, and carry a price tag of hundreds of millions of dollars. Smaller operations, such as municipal swimming pools or skating rinks, are typically found in parks and run by local authorities. The larger and more complex the sites, the more skills it can take to run them. "You are sort of a jack of all trades," says Lenny Willis, director of athletic facilities at the University of Illinois, whose responsibilities include the school's 62,800-seat Memorial Stadium. "It is good to know about electrical, plumbing, and architectural matters, and as many construction items as you can." As such, the job can be a study in multitasking. "I can be working on a budget one day," says Willis, a former National Football League player who supervises maintenance and cleanup crews that operate around the clock. "And if grass needs cutting the next day, I can do that too, as well as operate a forklift."

Essential Gear

Have knowledge of regulations and security requirements. Managers must ensure that stadiums and other sports venues comply with federal, state, and local regulations and employ effective security measures. For example, the Department of Homeland Security advises university stadium managers to set up game-day command posts to receive and respond to reports of potential security problems. Other recommended security practices range from prohibiting parking beneath a stadium to monitoring gates, stands, and vendor areas with closed-circuit television cameras.

Stadium managers typically work 12 hours or more on Saturday game days. They arrive early in the morning to ensure that all is ready, help television crews set up cameras and equipment if the game is to be televised, and leave hours after the final play. Few details escape their scrutiny, from the condition of the playing field to the supply of paper towels in the restrooms. These managers participate in long-range planning in addition to running day-to-day activities. They may consult about the design and construction of new facilities and the renovation of older ones, confer with builders, and negotiate with food vendors and other contractors.

Since owners want their sites to be used as often as possible in order to generate revenue, facility managers assist in arranging outside events and preparing year-round schedules. Events can range from high school and college basketball tournaments to rock concerts and road shows such as the Harlem Globetrotters and Holiday on Ice. Many parts of a facility can be used besides the playing field. The University of Illinois rents its stadium press box for wedding receptions, for example.

Facilities management calls for a careful eye for detail, along with leadership ability and analytical skills. Managers need to spot and head off possible maintenance problems and deal swiftly with those that arise. When preparing their budgets, managers must estimate the staffing requirements for games and other events, based on the expected size of crowds. The job requires both a patient disposition and willingness to take suggestions, as well as an ability to discern what demands must be addressed immediately versus those that can be addressed over time.

Typical job requirements include a bachelor's degree in sports management or a related subject, and often a master's degree as well. Employers may also want to see several years of experience in sports management or an allied field. While certificates are not a formal job requirement, they can serve as a stamp of approval. The International Facility Management Association offers a Facility Management Professional credential for entry-level workers, and a Certified Facility Manager credential for people already in the field. The latter requires a written examination and must be maintained through continuing education. Job listings are available on the association's Web site. Also providing certificates is the International Association of Assembly Managers, which represents managers of stadiums and other facilities, and posts news of jobs and internships on its site. The association's Certified Facilities Executive certificate requires a written test and an oral interview; managers who make the grade must be recertified every three years.

Essential Gear

Stock a good tool kit. Sports facility management can be both a desk job and a hands-on occupation. While managers employ maintenance and repair staffs, they can also choose to do physical work themselves. A familiarity with construction and the tools that it requires can help managers spot problems and see that they are fixed.

Facilities management jobs are expected to grow about as fast as average from 2006 to 2016, according to the U.S. Bureau of Labor Statistics (BLS), which lists the positions under the broad category of "administrative services managers." However, jobs in the subgroup that includes sports facility managers are projected to grow much faster than average. Attractive wages are available throughout this broad category, according to the BLS. It reported a median salary of $73,520 in 2008, with the top 10 percent of managers earning at least $129,700, and the bottom 10 percent making up to $37,400.

You Are Here

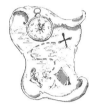

Determine your interest and ability to be a sports facility manager.

Do you enjoy multitasking? Sports facilities are complex structures that accommodate the needs of players, coaches, the media, and others, and may hold tens of thousands of spectators for games and events. Overseeing the numerous tasks that it takes to run such facilities smoothly is akin to juggling many balls at once. Effective managers are up to the challenge and enjoy the work.

Do you have strong communication skills? In a typical day, facility managers may deal with a wide range of people. Managers should be as comfortable when meeting with architects, administrators, and event

Navigating the Terrain

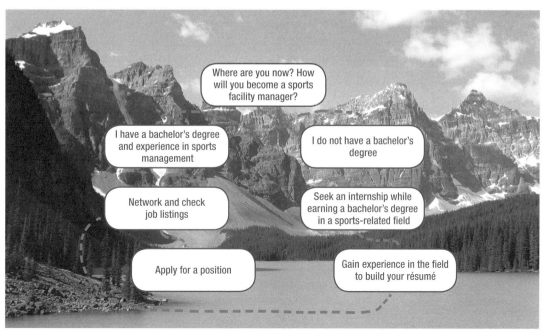

Where are you now? How will you become a sports facility manager?

I have a bachelor's degree and experience in sports management

I do not have a bachelor's degree

Network and check job listings

Seek an internship while earning a bachelor's degree in a sports-related field

Apply for a position

Gain experience in the field to build your résumé

planners as they are when instructing maintenance workers, ushers, and security guards. The ability to communicate clearly and effectively with diverse individuals is closely linked to the knack for multitasking that the position requires.

Are you a problem-solver? Without constant oversight, stadiums and arenas can quickly become problems waiting to happen. Defects can be anything from crumbling brick and mortar to heating and ventilation glitches that melt hockey ice. Part of the facility manager's job is to prevent and cope with day-to-day and long-term problems. This calls for the same type of foresight and planning skills that good managers employ when drawing up annual budgets and preparing stadiums and staffs for game days.

Organizing Your Expedition

Before you set out, know where you are going.

Decide on a destination. The sports management field is broad, and running sports facilities is just one of its many occupations. This means that you can reach your destination from a number of paths that may include marketing, finance, public relations, and event coordination. And since major university and professional sports facilities can have sizeable staffs, they may offer numerous opportunities to gain the experience that it takes to become a manager.

Scout the terrain. Graduates of sports administration programs typically enter the facility management field by way of internships they held in school. But for career changers who are out of school, this may not be possible. They should look for opportunities to apply the skills they already have to positions connected with operating facilities. This calls for networking and checking help-wanted listings in newspapers and online sites that include those of organizations that certify facility managers.

Find the path that's right for you. Once you have used your skills to gain a position, you can take on different tasks to broaden your experience. If your job is marketing the site as a venue for events, for example, you could try to expand your role to dealing with food vendors. The next

Notes from the Field
Stephen S. Showers
Associate vice president, facilities management, Towson University
Towson, Maryland

What were you doing before you decided to change careers?

I was in Student Affairs as a director of Housing, Food Service, and Residence Life at West Virginia University.

Why did you change your career?

An opportunity opened at West Virginia to become assistant vice president for facilities and services. Since I was responsible for the facilities management of a large residential system at West Virginia, I decided to apply for the position. It would be a promotion and be in an area of interest to me.

How did you make the transition?

Very easily. I knew the people at the institution, had ideas for improvements to the facilities management program, and worked well with the various departments that comprised the facilities management group at West Virginia.

What are the keys to success in your new career?

There are numerous nuances, but essentially the following are important. My student affairs background was very useful in understanding the needs and agendas with students, faculty, and staff. I always worked at hiring the best staff that I could find. With respect to managing sports facilities, my staff is responsible for all design, construction, and renovation of the sports and athletic facilities for the campus. In addition, we handle the regular maintenance and related operation of the facilities. The athletic department has its own facility manager who handles or coordinates the specialty work for the department.

I do not micromanage people. I give guidance and let staff take ownership of the project or problems to be solved. Listen! There are a lot of good ideas out there. Show appreciation for work that is well done. I have found that it is very worthwhile to spend time to follow up on issues and projects. It is amazing what falls through the cracks. Lastly, have fun and show that you enjoy what you and the organization are doing and accomplishing—it is infectious and makes the workplace much more enjoyable.

step could be a job as an assistant facility manager and the opportunity to work for advancement. Earning a certificate can improve your prospects.

Landmarks

If you are in your twenties . . . People who are already in sports management can seek out opportunities to work in athletic facilities. Early-career changers who are not in sports management, but who have marketing, administrative, or other experience, can parlay it into entry-level facility management positions or related jobs that can lead to such posts. At the same time, they can earn an entry-level facilities manager certificate to demonstrate the seriousness of their intent.

If you are in your thirties or forties . . . Mid-career changers who have worked in corporate sales or in event or construction management may enter the field at higher levels than younger people who are just starting out. Timing can be an important factor. For example, a construction manager could become a key assistant or associate facility manager by arriving when a new stadium or major renovation is being planned. In the same way, an experienced sales manager can be a valuable addition to the facilities staff when a big marketing push is in progress.

If you are in your fifties . . . Again, look for opportunities with construction or renovation efforts of major sports facilities. Senior career changers could be in an even better position to land jobs because of the contacts they have established over the years. However, such people may have less chance to advance to a top management role since their tenure will probably be shorter.

If you are over sixty . . . Part-time or volunteer work could be your most likely entry point. Do not be shy about making inquiries, particularly if you love sports. Stadium and arena staffs swell on game days, and you can make contacts and show your interest by taking an usher or ticket-taker job. That may open the door to working as a marketer or employing other skills that you have developed in your career.

Further Resources

The **International Association of Assembly Managers** certifies facilities managers and posts job listings and internships on its Web site. http://www.iaam.org

The **International Facility Management Association** provides entry-level and advanced certificates, posts job listings on its Web site, and publishes *Facility Management Journal* and *Today's Facility Manager* magazine. http://www.ifma.org

Scout

Scout

Career Compasses

Here is the breakdown of what it takes to be a successful sports scout.

Relevant Knowledge of the sport which you are scouting (40%)

Organizational Skills to rate players' performances and compare them with one another (20%)

Communication Skills to inform coaches and athletes of a player's prospects and abilities (20%)

Caring about the success of teams and athletes (20%)

Destination: Scout

Sports scouts are talent spotters who find and evaluate promising prospects for college and professional teams. Many begin as part-time freelancers and then land full-time jobs. Scouts also study a team's opponents to learn their strengths and weaknesses before upcoming games.

Scouts can work for a variety of employers in addition to professional teams. Some join combines that gather player information for a league or a group of professional teams. Others work for independent recruiting organizations that sign up high school athletes and bring them to the attention of college coaches. Still others are affiliated with online services that rate top high school and college players for audiences that include teams and sports fans.

Many scouts have played sports in college or the professional ranks; others have been coaches. College coaches generally double as scouts and draw on the knowledge of independent recruiters and information available on Web sites to help evaluate high school players. Scouting players requires a deep knowledge of sports and a sharp eye for talent and athletic potential. Scouts need to be detail-oriented and well organized to rate players, and need to be good communicators to discuss the pros and cons of athletes with coaches and others.

Essential Gear

Know your way around the Internet. While scouts travel widely, the Web has brought vast sums of information about high school and college athletes to personal computers. Newsletters, data, and multimedia profiles of players in action are all just a mouse-click away. Scouts can go online to see how other scouts rank players. Recruiters can send e-mail to prospects and view them on social networks. Scouts can also use Web sites to attract viewers and sign up high school athletes who hope to play in college.

Scouts gather information in many ways. They frequently travel to games and practices and may make several trips to evaluate a single player. Baseball and other sports hold showcase events where talented players perform before numerous scouts. A wealth of information is also available on Web sites like Scout.com and on social networks like Youtube.com that display the talents of high school and college athletes.

When scouting upcoming opponents, colleges use video departments to record the opposing team's games for coaches to review. Professional teams prepare in a similar manner. Coaches study what the opponent does in game situations, such as defending passing plays in football, and devise ways to counter the tactics.

The globalization of sports has widened the search for talent, sending scouts for professional teams abroad to hunt for promising players. Speaking a foreign language can be helpful. Japan, South Korea, and

Latin American countries produce major league baseball players, and the rosters of National Basketball Association teams include athletes from Europe, China, and Latin America.

Scouts who recommend high school players to colleges read sports pages and Web sites and talk with coaches. Some scouts may visit community hangouts to find out the players that students are talking about. Others operate Web sites that invite high school stars to sign up with them. Scouts evaluate everything from a high school athlete's physique to his or her work ethic. Since many teenagers are still growing, scouts must anticipate their development. Scouts then contact college coaches to recommend players who fit their programs.

Essential Gear

Be competent with statistics. Every sport is filled with statistics that scouts can use when gauging an athlete's performance and potential. Whether the numbers reflect a baseball pitcher's earned run average or a football player's yards per carry, scouts need to know what they mean and how to compile and use them. This can be essential when comparing players with one another. But scouts must also keep such numbers in perspective, since key qualities like an athlete's determination and work ethic cannot be easily measured.

Scouts for professional teams work closely with colleges. They attend football, basketball, and other practices and take in games as spectators. Such scouts may represent individual teams or combines like The National, which work on behalf of 18 members of the National Football League. These scouts deliver reports that help teams decide which players to draft.

Major league baseball employs the most scouts, including many freelancers. Scouts for teams attend local high school, college, and summer league games and file reports for their teams to use when drafting players. Other scouts track minor league players. Still others watch their team's next opponent play games and carefully chart the action.

The U.S. Bureau of Labor Statistics (BLS) lumps coaches and scouts into a single category that the agency says will grow at a faster-than-average pace for the 10-year period that ends in 2016. (See Chapter 1: Coaches and Sports Instructors for the combined wage data.) Most new jobs will be for coaches, according to the BLS, though people who want to work as scouts will find many options open.

You Are Here

Determine your interest and ability to become a sports scout.

Have you played or coached a sport? Scouts who have done one or both are likely to bring a thorough knowledge of their sport and a sharp eye for talent to the job. Experience as a college team manager can also provide good training for work as a scout. However, people who simply love a sport and know a good deal about it can succeed if they are willing to put in the time and hard work that are needed to assess a player's physical skills and mental and emotional qualities.

Can you recognize talent? Scouts stand or fall on their ability to spot the ingredients of success in individual athletes. Scouting is highly competitive; those scouts whose picks disappoint, or who regularly overlook good players, are unlikely to advance in the field. But scouts who recognize potential in an athlete that other scouts miss can become highly sought after for advice and counsel. This is true both for scouts employed by teams and for individuals who set up Web sites to rate college and professional prospects.

Do you like to travel? Scouting calls for attending practices and games to get to know players and watch them perform. While film and videotape may be available, there is no substitute for a first-hand view of athletes on the court or field. This typically means traveling to high school and college games that are held throughout the parts of the country that scouts are assigned to cover. Scouts for professional teams travel throughout the country and frequently go abroad as well.

Organizing Your Expedition

Before you set out, know where you are going.

Decide on a destination. Scouts are intelligence agents who can work for teams or scouting organizations or go into business for themselves. Your first task is to become knowledgeable about one or more sport and to develop an eye for talent. Next, consider what type of employer you want to work for, or whether to branch out on your own. Whichever

Navigating the Terrain

direction you choose, keep in mind that scouting is a competitive and specialized occupation. It requires hard work to gain the insight and skills that it takes to set yourself apart from the rest.

Scout the terrain. Different scouts address different audiences. Those working for teams or combines prepare reports solely for that team or combine, while those with organizations like Scout.com provide information that is followed largely by sports fans and also used by teams. Breaking into either type of work can be difficult, and newcomers should network with coaches and scouting organizations to demonstrate their knowledge and judgment. Aspiring scouts generally start at the grassroots level by studying local athletes and passing along tips about their abilities.

Find the path that's right for you. Newcomers typically create their own paths in this field. People who want to work for professional teams need to become familiar with the year-round scouting schedules that lead to annual drafts. For example, major league baseball scouts rate

Notes from the Field

Bob Johnson
New York Mets baseball scout
Sarasota, Florida

What were you doing before you decided to change careers?

I was a high school social studies teacher for 25 years. I taught and scouted for a long time together. A lot of scouts have been teachers because they have their summers off.

Why did you change your career?

I was at the spot where I could file for a pension and go into something that I have always loved, which was baseball. I had been a freelance scout during the summer and I was offered a good opportunity.

How did you make the transition?

It was pretty seamless. In the job I moved into I could live in the same place but I traveled a lot, since scouts go all over the country. And without the Monday-through-Friday teaching gig I could do that.

What are the keys to success in your new career?

Hard work and attention to detail and willingness to do whatever it takes to do the job. As an advance scout, I stay about a week ahead of our big-league team. My job is to prepare the team to play against the next opponent. I try to find weaknesses in the opponent's pitchers for our hitters to exploit, and weaknesses in the opponent's hitters that our pitchers can take advantage of. The job is very intense. I really have to bear down to follow each pitch and cannot afford to engage in conversation. The job is also specialized. Most scouts are involved in scouting free agents, looking for trades, and things like that. I basically am trying to get our major league team ready to play the opposition.

The most important thing in our industry is for a person to understand that the game is bigger than any of us, and to have respect for what we do. I have a very specific job and try to do it to the best of my ability. You as an individual are not the reason for a team's success. There's no room for ego. A little humility goes a long way in this field.

high school and college players during the school year to prepare for the June draft. Career changers can help by developing information for the scouts to use. Scouting then shifts to summer-league games that offer the opportunity for further work, which can be an especially valuable time for teachers who have their summers off. Professional football, basketball, and hockey teams likewise scout promising players throughout the school year. Aspiring scouts may work in a similar way with online sites that evaluate athletes before professional drafts and during college recruiting seasons.

Landmarks

If you are in your twenties . . . You may be poised to begin a transition to scouting, especially if you have played a sport or been a team manager in college. Now is the time to make contacts, gain experience, and develop your skills as a talent-spotter. Whether or not you have played sports yourself, there is no substitute for spending hours at local gyms and fields to study athletes and their teams. You can then deliver well-informed opinions about a player's prospects, and build a reputation for being indispensable.

If you are in your thirties or forties . . . Retired athletes often go into scouting at this age. People who coach or who love a sport may now seek part-time jobs as scouts for professional teams that can lead to full-time work. Those who are fans of high school sports may collect information that college coaches and online scouting organizations find useful and that can lead to scouting jobs.

If you are in your fifties . . . While part-time scouting remains an option, full-time scouts are generally well established by now. For people who have run a business, this may be the time to set up your own Web site as a scout or recruiter—especially if a favorite sport remains a passion for you. People who follow this route can find building such a site a natural way to blend their interest in sports with their entrepreneurial skills.

If you are over sixty . . . Scouting is an occupation in which judgment can improve with age. Senior scouts are less likely to be dazzled by a prospect's flashy moves or headlines than a younger scout might be.

Older scouts also may pay closer attention to qualities like a strong work ethic that are vital to an athlete's long-term success. For avid sports fans that have retired or are near retirement from their regular jobs, scouting can become an enjoyable part-time vocation.

Further Resources

The **NFL Scouting Combine** holds an annual weeklong tryout for top college football players and posts the results on its Web site, showing the skills that professional football scouts evaluate.   http://www.nfl.com/combine **Scout.com** provides news and information about top high school and college players.   http://www.scout.com

Sports Event Manager

Sports Event Manager

Career Compasses

Here is the breakdown of what it takes to become a sports event manager.

Organizational Skills to plan and carry out events (30%)

Communication Skills to coordinate the roles of groups and individuals (30%)

Relevant Knowledge of the events you are managing (20%)

Caring about the needs of participants and clients (20%)

Destination: Sports Event Manager

Event managers make things happen. They plan and run everything from global extravaganzas like the summer Olympics to local five-kilometer charity races. Some managers work for facilities such as stadiums or arenas that host events. Others work for large international companies that provide assistance at such venues, or partner with corporate clients to create their own events. Still others run small companies that organize community activities that bring together athletes, fans, and sponsors that provide revenue. Many managers work directly with sports groups that organize big events. For example, the U.S. Golf Association hires MSG Promotions of Bethlehem, Pennsylvania, to sell corporate sponsorships and manage hospitality suites for the annual U.S. Open Championship.

Event managers are both far-sighted and detail-oriented. They start by drafting an overall plan and then prepare schedules, assign duties, and make preparations for when things go wrong. They are careful to parcel out jobs to those who can handle them. "You do not want to put someone lacking in personality and confidence in charge of the VIP or media check-in table," says Michael Neuman, president of Amplify Sports and Entertainment, an event management company in New York City. The larger and more complex an event, the more people a manager may work with. A typical team can include facilities directors, marketing and public relations specialists, and box office and ticket personnel. Event managers coordinate all these individuals, anticipate problems, and work to stay on schedule. Keeping everything on track requires patience, diligence, and a high degree of organization. A sense of humor also helps, as does remaining cool under pressure; buckling under stress can damage morale and thwart progress.

Essential Gear

Know the terms. *Comps* is the short term for "complimentary tickets." These are tickets that events give away in order to fill seats when sales have been slow. This is normally done as a last resort and is commonly known as "papering the house." The acronym *VIK* stands for "value in kind" goods and services that sponsors provide in lieu of cash. For example, an oil company that sponsors a motor race might provide oil and gasoline for the event. In the same way, a sports drink maker could provide beverages to runners or bicyclists in road races, or to participants in football or basketball youth clinics.

Planning events calls for working with sponsors who provide the revenue to run them. Companies can be eager to participate since sports events make good advertising venues. Take the 2009 Wimbledon tennis tournament in London, England: No fewer than 14 companies provided everything from the official tennis balls to the official bottled water and the official ice cream—and paid handsomely for the right to do so. This enabled the All England Lawn Tennis and Croquet Club, which hosts the tournament, to generate a profit from the event and plow the money into the development of British tennis.

The art of wooing sponsors includes creating benefit packages. Typical benefits include hospitality suites for sponsors and their guests, parties before and after events, and prominent use of a sponsor's name on programs. Title sponsors can have entire events, such as the FedEx Orange Bowl and the Tostitos Fiesta Bowl, named after them. Managers also create events for individual sponsors. For example, Amplify Sports and Entertainment put together a celebrity flag football game for a client to raise awareness of its role as a National Football League partner. The game, held in connection with the start of the NFL season, garnered widespread media coverage.

Essential Gear

Be prepared for post-event analysis. Once an event has been completed, managers and clients sit down to assess how well it has met their revenue goals and other objectives. Criteria can include the amount of attention the event has received in terms of paid attendance, the size of the radio and television audience if broadcast rights have been sold, and the extent of news coverage. But since companies use sponsorships for different purposes, there are no one-size-fits-all criteria for measuring success. Managers might randomly survey stadium crowds before and after an event, for example, to see if their perception of the sponsor has changed. Software can measure the amount of television exposure a sponsor's stadium sign gets by breaking up broadcasts into a series of images and computing how long the sign was seen on camera; this helps sponsors assess their return on investment.

Most event-management jobs require a degree from a four-year college. Useful majors include sports management, business administration, marketing, and public relations. Student internships are available from event-management companies and organizations such as the Big Ten Conference, golf's PGA Tour, and the U.S. Soccer Federation. In addition, many universities offer internships in their athletic departments. Since events can take a great many people to run, volunteer opportunities are plentiful. Volunteers may do everything from assisting with marketing programs to answering phones and welcoming athletes.

Sports event managers can earn handsome wages, especially if they oversee big events. The U.S. Bureau of Labor Statistics (BLS) includes sports event managers in the category "Advertising and Promotion Managers," for which the median annual salary was $80,220 in 2008. The top 10 percent of individuals in this category made at least $166,400 a year, while the bottom 10 percent earned up to $40,090. The category as a whole is projected to grow more slowly than average between 2006 and 2016, according to the BLS, but jobs for event promoters are expected to grow much faster than average over the same stretch.

You Are Here

Determine your interest and ability to be a sports event manager.

Are you articulate and highly organized? These are key qualities for anyone who wants to manage or participate in the management of sports events. Even relatively small community events call for handling numerous details and working with many people. Big events typically involve a bewildering number of details to master under deadline pressure, and countless individuals and groups to oversee. All this takes the ability to communicate clearly and maintain constant vigilance, as well as knowing when to supervise and when to delegate.

Navigating the Terrain

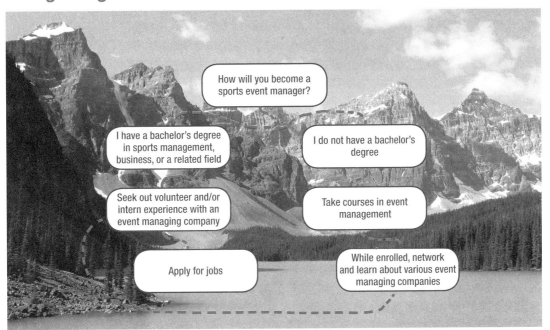

How will you become a sports event manager?

I have a bachelor's degree in sports management, business, or a related field

I do not have a bachelor's degree

Seek out volunteer and/or intern experience with an event managing company

Take courses in event management

Apply for jobs

While enrolled, network and learn about various event managing companies

How creative are you? Besides handling myriad details, sports event managers are called upon to develop creative solutions to a wide range of client needs and logistical problems. These can range from fashioning an entire event to focus attention on a sponsor's brand, to designing strategies to attract and manage crowds. Good sports event managers are creative thinkers and effective implementers at the same time.

Can you bounce back from setbacks? Event managers face the constant risk of things going wrong. Setbacks can be anything from rain on the event day to last-minute decisions by a sponsor or key participant to pull out. Event managers must foresee and prepare for such possibilities, and remain calm and poised when the unexpected occurs. The measure of good managers is not only how they perform when things go smoothly, but also how well they are able to overcome obstacles.

Organizing Your Expedition

Before you set out, know where you are going.

Decide on a destination. The vast number and variety of sports events that are held each year provides a wealth of opportunities to enter the field. Career changers can work for an event-management company, a sports facility or organization that holds sports events, or go into business for themselves. If you have played a sport in high school or college, or enjoy activities such as tennis or golf, the experience can be helpful in deciding the direction in which to go. The key point is to pick a destination that makes the best use of your interest and skills.

Scout the terrain. So many sports events take place around the country that there is bound to be one near you. Fund-raisers such as runs and walks for charity are held throughout the year and provide opportunities to volunteer and test your interest in event management. You can contact event managers at local sports facilities to get a feel for the challenges and rewards of this type of work. At the same time, check newspaper and online job listings for job openings and look into internship possibilities.

Find the path that's right for you. Since event management encompasses many disciplines, there are numerous ways to apply your skills.

Notes from the Field

Jim Young
Owner, Young & Associates, a sports event management firm
Raleigh, North Carolina

What were you doing before you decided to change careers?

I was in the insurance business.

Why did you change your career?

I was a lousy salesperson. I hated cold calling and making calls. Now people call me.

How did you make the transition?

I was a cross-country runner in high school and college and I directed my first race in 1981 for the local running club. People would come to my races and say, "Could you help me with races?" The insurance business lifted gradually. Each year my income from insurance got less and my income from races grew more. In 1989 I left insurance and set up my company.

What is the secret to success in your new career?

You have got to be service-oriented and willing to work hard. I see myself as a service company. People are looking for a large number of people to attend events so the events can make money. By placing the event on several running Web sites and distributing entry forms at races preceding the race, I can get the word out to the running community. I wrote a letter this year to all my event clients to say that since the economy was down, I was going to lower my price. I got a great response, and that is what I think it means to be a service company.

Besides deciding *where* you want to work, you can choose *what* work you want to do. If you have a background in sales, for example, selling sponsorships might be the path for you. Or if you have managed a conference center or restaurant, setting up and running hospitality suites could be a good fit. Since you are unlikely to vault into an overall event manager's job without considerable experience, you will want to leverage the know-how that you have as a way to get started.

Landmarks

If you are in your twenties . . . Internships and volunteer work are in order if you have a college degree. If not, take courses and workshops to gain knowledge of sports event management, and make contacts in the field. Create a checklist of all the skills that are needed to manage events and emphasize those that you have when putting together your résumé.

If you are in your thirties or forties . . . Even if you have never worked in sports, you may have plenty of experience that employers who are looking for event managers can use. A proven ability to handle many details at once is a basic requirement, and demonstrated sales, marketing, and planning skills are highly useful. Volunteer and part-time work will provide the chance to show what abilities you possess and how well you can use them.

If you are in your fifties . . . Many of the same principles for those in their thirties and forties apply to you. The contacts and relevant skills that you have developed can make you especially attractive to employers seeking seasoned individuals who can cope with problems with a steady hand.

If you are over sixty . . . Volunteering or working for community-based events will enable you to make use of your skills and draw on relationships that you have built over the years with neighbors and friends. Since many community events have the goal of raising money for charities, this will also enable you to contribute time and effort on behalf of a good cause.

Further Resources

Sports event management organizations **Amplify Sports and Entertainment, Octagon,** and **IMG World** all list job openings for event managers and post information about internships on their respective Web sites. http://www.ampfirm.com, http://www.octagonna.com, and http://www.imgworld.com

The **PGA Tour** offers full-time paid internships lasting from 10 to 12 weeks. http://www.pgatour.com/company/internships.html

The **U.S. Soccer Federation** provides online information about internship opportunities. http://www.ussoccer.com

Appendix A

Going Solo: Starting Your Own Business

Starting your own business can be very rewarding—not only in terms of potential financial success, but also in the pleasure derived from building something from the ground up, contributing to the community, being your own boss, and feeling reasonably in control of your fate. However, business ownership carries its own obligations—both in terms of long hours of hard work and new financial and legal responsibilities. If you succeed in growing your business, your responsibilities only increase. Many new business owners come in expecting freedom only to find themselves chained tighter to their desks than ever before. Still, many business owners find greater satisfaction in their career paths than do workers employed by others.

The Internet has also changed the playing field for small business owners, making it easier than ever before to strike out on your own. While small mom-and-pop businesses such as hairdressers and grocery stores have always been part of the economic landscape, the Internet has made reaching and marketing to a niche easier and more profitable. This has made possible a boom in *microbusinesses*. Generally, a microbusiness is considered to have under ten employees. A microbusiness is also sometimes called a *SOHO* for "small office/home office."

The following appendix is intended to explain, in general terms, the steps in launching a small business, no matter whether it is selling your Web-design services or opening a pizzeria with business partners. It will also point out some of the things you will need to bear in mind. Remember also that the particular obligations of your municipality, state, province, or country may vary, and that this is by no means a substitute for doing your own legwork. Further suggested reading is listed at the end.

Crafting a Business Plan

It has often been said that success is 1 percent inspiration and 99 percent perspiration. However, the interface between the two can often be hard to achieve. The first step to taking your idea and making it reality is constructing a viable *business plan*. The purpose of a business plan is to think things all the way through, to make sure your ideas really are profitable, and to figure out the "who, what, when, where, why, and how" of your business. It fills in the details for three areas: your goals, why you think they are attainable, and how you plan to get to there. "You need to know where you're going before you take that first step," says Drew Curtis, successful Internet entrepreneur and founder of the popular newsfilter Fark.com.

Take care in writing your business plan. Generally, these documents contain several parts: An *executive summary* stating the essence of the plan; a *market summary* explaining how a need exists for the product and service you will supply and giving an idea of potential profitability by comparing your business to similar organizations; a *company description* which includes your products and services, why you think your organization will succeed, and any special advantages you have, as well as a description of *organization* and *management*; and your *marketing and sales strategy*. This last item should include market highlights and demographic information and trends that relate to your proposal. Also include a *funding request* for the amount of start-up capital you will need. This is supported by a section on *financials*, or the sort of cash flow you can expect, based on market analysis, projection, and comparison with existing companies. Other needed information, such as personal financial history, résumés, legal documents, or pictures of your product, can be placed in *appendices*.

Use your business plan to get an idea of how much startup money is necessary and to discipline your thinking and challenge your preconceived notions before you develop your cash flow. The business plan will tell you how long it will take before you turn a profit, which in turn is linked to how long it will before you will be able to pay back investors or a bank loan—which is something that anyone supplying you with money will want to know. Even if you are planning to subsist on grants or you are not planning on investment or even starting a for-profit company, the discipline imposed by the business plan is still the first step to organizing your venture.

A business plan also gives you a realistic view of your personal financial obligations. How long can you afford to live without regular income? How are you going to afford medical insurance? When will your business begin turning a profit? How much of a profit? Will you need to reinvest your profits in the business, or can you begin living off of them? Proper planning is key to success in any venture.

A final note on business plans: Take into account realistic expected profit minus realistic costs. Many small business owners begin by underestimating start-ups and variable costs (such as electricity bills), and then underpricing their product. This effectively paints them into a corner from which it is hard to make a profit. Allow for realistic market conditions on both the supply and the demand side.

Partnering Up

You should think long and hard about the decision to go into business with a partner (or partners). Whereas other people can bring needed capital, expertise, and labor to a business, they can also be liabilities. The questions you need to ask yourself are:

☞ Will this person be a full and equal partner? In other words, are they able to carry their own weight? Make a full and fair assessment of your potential partner's personality. Going into business with someone who lacks a work ethic, or prefers giving directions to working in the trenches, can be a frustrating experience.

☞ What will they contribute to the business? For instance, a partner may bring in start-up money, facilities, or equipment. However, consider if this is enough of a reason to bring them on board. You may be able to get the same advantages in another way—for instance, renting a garage rather than working out of your partner's. Likewise, doubling skill sets does not always double productivity.

☞ Do they have any liabilities? For instance, if your prospective partner has declared bankruptcy in the past, this can hurt your collective venture's ability to get credit.

☞ Will the profits be able to sustain all the partners? Many start-up ventures do not turn profits immediately, and what little they do produce can be spread thin amongst many partners. Carefully work out the math.

Also bear in mind that going into business together can put a strain on even the best personal relationships. No matter whether it is family, friends, or strangers, keep everything very professional with written agreements regarding these investments. Get everything in writing, and be clear where obligations begin and end. "It's important to go into business with the right people," says Curtis. "If you don't—if it degrades into infighting and petty bickering—it can really go south quickly."

Incorporating. . . or Not

Think long and hard about incorporating. Starting a business often requires a fairly large—and risky—financial investment, which in turn exposes you to personal liability. Furthermore, as your business grows, so does your risk. Incorporating can help you shield yourself from this liability. However, it also has disadvantages.

To begin with, incorporating is not necessary for conducting professional transactions such as obtaining bank accounts and credit. You can do this as a sole proprietor, partnership, or simply by filing a DBA ("doing business as") statement with your local court (also known as "trading as" or an "assumed business name"). The DBA is an accounting entity that facilitates commerce and keeps your business' money separate from your own. However, the DBA does not shield you from responsibility if your business fails. It is entirely possible to ruin your credit, lose your house, and have your other assets seized in the unfortunate event of bankruptcy.

The purpose of incorporating is to shield yourself from personal financial liability. In case the worst happens, only the business' assets can be taken. However, this is not always the best solution. Check your local laws: Many states have laws that prevent a creditor from seizing a non-incorporated small business' assets in case of owner bankruptcy. If you are a corporation, however, the things you use to do business that are owned by the corporation—your office equipment, computers, restaurant refrigerators, and other essential equipment—may be seized by creditors, leaving you no way to work yourself out of debt. This is why it is imperative to consult with a lawyer.

There are other areas in which being a corporation can be an advantage, such as business insurance. Depending on your business needs, insurance can be for a variety of things: malpractice, against delivery failures or spoilage, or liability against defective products or accidents. Furthermore, it is easier to hire employees, obtain credit, and buy health insurance as an organization than as an individual. However, on the downside, corporations are subject to specific and strict laws concerning management and ownership. Again, you should consult with a knowledgeable legal expert.

Among the things you should discuss with your legal expert are the advantages and disadvantages of incorporating in your jurisdiction and which type of incorporation is best for you. The laws on liability and how much of your profit will be taken away in taxes vary widely by state and country. Generally, most small businesses owners opt for *limited liability companies* (LLCs), which gives them more control and a more flexible management structure. (Another possibility is a *limited liability partnership*, or *LLP*, which is especially useful for professionals such as doctors and lawyers.) Finally, there is the *corporation*, which is characterized by transferable ownerships shares, perpetual succession, and, of course, limited liability.

Most small businesses are sole proprietorships, partnerships, or privately-owned corporations. In the past, not many incorporated, since it was necessary to have multiple owners to start a corporation. However, this is changing, since it is now possible in many states for an individual to form a corporation. Note also that the form your business takes is usually not set in stone: A sole proprietorship or partnership can switch to become an LLC as it grows and the risks increase; furthermore, a successful LLC can raise capital by changing its structure to become a corporation and selling stock.

Legal Issues

Many other legal issues besides incorporating (or not) need to be addressed before you start your business. It is impossible to speak directly to every possible business need in this brief appendix, since regulations, licenses, and health and safety codes vary by industry and locality. A restaurant in Manhattan, for instance, has to deal not only with the usual issues such as health inspectors, and the state liquor board, but obscure regulations such as New York City's cabaret laws, which prohibit dancing without a license in a place where alcohol is sold. An asbestos-abatement company, on the other hand, has a very different set of standards it has to abide by, including federal regulations. Researching applicable laws is part of starting up any business.

Part of being a wise business owner is knowing when you need help. There is software available for things like bookkeeping, business plans, and Web site creation, but generally, consulting with a knowledgeable professional—an accountant or a lawyer (or both)—is the smartest move. One of the most common mistakes is believing that just because you have expertise in the technical aspects of a certain field, you know all about running a business in that field. Whereas some people may balk at the expense, by suggesting the best way to deal with possible problems, as well as cutting through red tape and seeing possible pitfalls that you may not even have been aware of, such professionals usually more than make up for their cost. After all, they have far more experience at this than does a first-time business owner!

Financial

Another necessary first step in starting a business is obtaining a bank account. However, having the account is not as important as what you do with it. One of the most common problems with small businesses is undercapitalization—especially in brick-and-mortar businesses that sell or make something, rather than service-based businesses. The rule of thumb is that you should have access to money equal to your first year's anticipated profits, plus start-up expenses. (Note that this is not the same as having the money on hand—see the discussion on lines of credit, below.) For instance, if your annual rent, salaries, and equipment will cost $50,000 and you expect $25,000 worth of profit in your first year, you should have access to $75,000 worth of financing.

You need to decide what sort of financing you will need. Small business loans have both advantages and disadvantages. They can provide critical start-up credit, but in order to obtain one, your personal credit will need to be good, and you will, of course, have to pay them off with interest. In general, the more you and your partners put into the business yourselves, the more credit lenders will be willing to extend to you.

Equity can come from your own personal investment, either in cash or an equity loan on your home. You may also want to consider bringing on partners—at least limited financial partners—as a way to cover start-up costs.

It is also worth considering obtaining a line of credit instead of a loan. A loan is taken out all at once, but with a line of credit, you draw on the money as you need it. This both saves you interest payments and means that you have the money you need when you need it. Taking out too large of a loan can be worse than having no money at all! It just sits there collecting interest—or, worse, is spent on something utterly unnecessary—and then is not around when you need it most.

The first five years are the hardest for any business venture; your venture has about double the usual chance of closing in this time (1 out of 6, rather than 1 out of 12). You will probably have to tighten your belt at home, as well as work long hours and keep careful track of your business expenses. Be careful with your money. Do not take unnecessary risks, play it conservatively, and always keep some capital in reserve for emergencies. The hardest part of a new business, of course, is the learning curve of figuring out what, exactly, you need to do to make a profit, and so the best advice is to have plenty of savings—or a job to provide income—while you learn the ropes.

One thing you should not do is count on venture capitalists or "angel investors," that is, businesspeople who make a living investing on other businesses in the hopes that their equity in the company will increase in value. Venture capitalists have gotten something of a reputation as indiscriminate spendthrifts due to some poor choices made during the dot-com boom of the late 1990s, but the fact is that most do not take risks on unproven products. Rather, they are attracted to young companies that have the potential to become regional or national powerhouses and give better-than-average returns. Nor are venture capitalists endless sources of money; rather, they are savvy businesspeople who are usually attracted to companies that have already experienced a measure of success. Therefore, it is better to rely on your own resources until you have proven your business will work.

Bookkeeping 101

The principles of double-entry bookkeeping have not changed much since its invention in the fifteenth century: one column records debits, and one records credits. The trick is *doing* it. As a small business owner, you need to be disciplined and meticulous at recording your finances. Thankfully, today there is software available that can do everything from tracking payables and receivables to running checks and generating reports.

Honestly ask yourself if you are the sort of person who does a good job keeping track of finances. If you are not, outsource to a bookkeeping company or hire someone to come in once or twice a week to enter invoices and generate checks for you. Also remember that if you have employees or even freelancers, you will have to file tax forms for them at the end of the year.

Another good idea is to have an accountant for your business to handle advice and taxes (federal, state, local, sales tax, etc.). In fact, consulting with a certified public accountant is a good idea in general, since they are usually aware of laws and rules that you have never even heard of.

Finally, keep your personal and business accounting separate. If your business ever gets audited, the first thing the IRS looks for is personal expenses disguised as business expenses. A good accountant can help you to know what are legitimate business expenses. Everything you take from the business account, such as payroll and reimbursement, must be recorded and classified.

Being an Employer

Know your situation regarding employees. To begin with, if you have any employees, you will need an Employer Identification Number (EIN), also sometimes called a Federal Tax Identification Number. Getting an EIN is simple: You can fill out IRS form SS-4, or complete the process online at http://www.irs.gov.

Having employees carries other responsibilities and legalities with it. To begin with, you will need to pay payroll taxes (otherwise known as "withholding") to cover income tax, unemployment insurance, Social Security, and Medicare, as well as file W-2 and W-4 forms with the government. You will also be required to pay worker's compensation insurance, and will probably also want to find medical insurance. You are also required to abide by your state's nondiscrimination laws. Most states require you to post nondiscrimination and compensation notices in a public area.

Many employers are tempted to unofficially hire workers "off the books." This can have advantages, but can also mean entering a legal gray area. (Note, however, this is different from hiring freelancers, a temp employed by another company, or having a self-employed professional such as an accountant or bookkeeper come in occasionally to provide a service.) It is one thing to hire the neighbor's teenage son on a one-time basis to help you move some boxes, but quite another to have full-time workers working on a cash-and-carry basis. Regular wages must be noted in the accounts, and gaps may be questioned in the event of an audit. If the workers are injured on the job, you are not covered by worker's comp, and are thus vulnerable to lawsuits. If the workers you hired are not legal residents, you can also be liable for civil and criminal penalties. In general, it is best to keep your employees as above-board as possible.

Building a Business

Good business practices are essential to success. First off, do not overextend yourself. Be honest about what you can do and in what time frame. Secondly, be a responsible business owner. In general, if there is a problem, it is best to explain matters honestly to your clients than to leave them without word and wondering. In the former case, there is at least the possibility of salvaging your reputation and credibility.

Most business is still built by personal contacts and word of mouth. It is for this reason that maintaining your list of contacts is an essential practice. Even if a particular contact may not be useful at a particular moment, a future opportunity may present itself—or you may be able to send someone else to them. Networking, in other words, is as important when you are the boss as when you are looking for a job yourself. As the owner of a company, having a network means getting services on better terms, knowing where to go if you need help with a particular problem, or simply being in the right place at the right time to exploit an opportunity. Join professional organizations, the local Chamber of Commerce, clubs and community organizations, and learn to play golf. And remember—never burn a bridge.

Advertising is another way to build a business. Planning an ad campaign is not as difficult as you might think: You probably already know your media market and business community. The trick is applying it. Again, go with your instincts. If you never look twice at your local weekly, other people probably do not, either. If you are in a high-tourist area, though, local tourist maps might be a good way to leverage your marketing dollar. Ask other people in your area or market who have businesses similar to your own. Depending on your focus, you might want to consider everything from AM radio or local TV networks, to national trade publications, to hiring a PR firm for an all-out blitz. By thinking about these questions, you can spend your advertising dollars most effectively.

Nor should you underestimate the power of using the Internet to build your business. It is a very powerful tool for small businesses, potentially reaching vast numbers of people for relatively little outlay of money. Launching a Web site has become the modern equivalent of hanging out your shingle. Even if you are primarily a brick-and-mortar business, a Web presence can still be an invaluable tool—your store or offices will show up on Google searches, plus customers can find directions to visit you in person. Furthermore, the Internet offers the small-business owner many useful tools. Print and design services, order fulfillment, credit card processing, and networking—both personal and in terms of linking to other sites—are all available online. Web advertising can be useful, too, either by advertising on specialty sites that appeal to your audience, or by using services such as Google AdWords.

Amateurish print ads, TV commercials, and Web sites do not speak well of your business. Good media should be well-designed, well-edited, and well-put together. It need not, however, be expensive. Shop around and, again, use your network.

Flexibility is also important. "In general, a business must adapt to changing conditions, find new customers and find new products or services that customers need when the demand for their older products or services diminishes," says James Peck, a Long Island, New York, entrepreneur. In other words, if your original plan is not working out, or if demand falls, see if you can parlay your experience, skills, and physical plant into meeting other needs. People are not the only ones who can change their path in life; organizations can, too.

A Final Word

In business, as in other areas of life, the advice of more experienced people is essential. "I think it really takes three businesses until you know what you're doing," Drew Curtis confides. "I sure didn't know what I was doing the first time." Listen to what others have to say, no matter whether it is about your Web site or your business plan. One possible solution is seeking out a mentor, someone who has previously launched a successful venture in this field. In any case, before taking any step, ask as many people as many questions as you can. Good advice is invaluable.

Further Resources

American Independent Business Alliance
http://www.amiba.net

American Small Business League
http://www.asbl.com

IRS Small Business and Self-Employed One-Stop Resource
http://www.irs.gov/businesses/small/index.html

The Riley Guide: Steps in Starting Your Own Business
http://www.rileyguide.com/steps.html

Small Business Administration
http://www.sba.gov

Appendix B

Outfitting Yourself for Career Success

As you contemplate a career shift, the first component is to assess your interests. You need to figure out what makes you tick, since there is a far greater chance that you will enjoy and succeed in a career that taps into your passions, inclinations, natural abilities, and training. If you have a general idea of what your interests are, you at least know in which direction you want to travel. You may know you want to simply switch from one sort of nursing to another, or change your life entirely and pursue a dream you have always held. In this case, you can use a specific volume of The Field Guides to Finding a New Career to discover which position to target. If you are unsure of the direction you want to take, well, then the entire scope of the series is open to you! Browse through to see what appeals to you, and see if it matches with your experience and abilities.

The next step you should take is to make a list—do it once in writing—of the skills you have used in a position of responsibility that transfer to the field you are entering. People in charge of interviewing and hiring may well understand that the skills they are looking for in a new hire are used in other fields, but you must spell it out. Most job descriptions are partly a list of skills. Map your experience into that, and very early in your contacts with a prospective employer explicitly address how you acquired your relevant skills. Pick a relatively unimportant aspect of the job to be your ready answer for where you would look forward to learning within the organization, if this seems essentially correct. When you transfer into a field, softly acknowledge a weakness while relating your readiness to learn, but never lose sight of the value you offer both in your abilities and in the freshness of your perspective.

Energy and Experience

The second component in career-switching success is energy. When Jim Fulmer was 61, he found himself forced to close his piano-repair business. However, he was able to parlay his knowledge of music, pianos, and the musical instruments industry into another job as a sales representative for a large piano manufacturer, and quickly built up a clientele of musical-instrument retailers throughout the East Coast. Fulmer's experience highlights another essential lesson for career-changers: There are plenty of opportunities out there, but jobs will not come to you—especially the career-oriented, well-paying ones. You have to seek them out.

Jim Fulmer's case also illustrates another important point: Former training and experience can be a key to success. "Anyone who has to make a career change in any stage of life has to look at what skills they have acquired but may not be aware of," he says. After all, people can more easily change into careers similar to the ones they are leaving. Training and experience also let you enter with a greater level of seniority, provided you have the other necessary qualifications. For instance, a nurse who is already experienced with administering drugs and their benefits and drawbacks, and who is also graced with the personality and charisma to work with the public, can become a pharmaceutical company sales representative.

Unlock Your Network

The next step toward unlocking the perfect job is networking. The term may be overused, but the idea is as old as civilization. More than other animals, humans need one another. With the Internet and telephone, never in history has it been easier to form (or revive) these essential links. One does not have to gird oneself and attend reunion-type events (though for many this is a fine tactic)—but keep open to opportunities to meet people who may be friendly to you in your field. Ben Franklin understood the principle well—*Poor Richard's Almanac* is something of a treatise on the importance of cultivating what Franklin called "friendships" with benefactors. So follow in the steps of the founding fathers and make friends to get ahead. Remember: helping others feels good; it's often the receiving that gets a little tricky. If you know someone particularly well-connected in your field, consider tapping one or two less important connections first so that you make the most of the important one. As you proceed, keep your strengths foremost in your mind because the glue of commerce is mutual interest.

Eighty percent of job openings are *never advertised*, and, according to the U.S. Bureau of Labor statistics, more than half of all employees landed their jobs through networking. Using your personal contacts is far more efficient and effective than trusting your résumé to the Web.

On the Web, an employer needs to sort through tens of thousands—or millions—of résumés. When you direct your application to one potential employer, you are directing your inquiry to one person who already knows you. The personal touch is everything: Human beings are social animals, programmed to "read" body language; we are naturally inclined to trust those we meet in person, or who our friends and coworkers have recommended. While Web sites can be useful (for looking through help-wanted ads, for instance), expecting employers to pick you out of the slush pile is as effective as throwing your résumé into a black hole.

Do not send your résumé out just to make yourself feel like you're doing something. The proper way to go about things is to employ discipline and order, and then to apply your charm. Begin your networking efforts by making a list of people you can talk to: colleagues, coworkers, and supervisors, people you have had working relationship with, people from church, athletic teams, political organizations, or other community groups, friends, and relatives. You can expand your networking opportunities by following the suggestions in each chapter of the volumes. Your goal here is not so much to land a job as to expand your possibilities and knowledge: Though the people on your list may not be in the position to help you themselves, they might know someone who is. Meeting with them might also help you understand traits that matter and skills that are valued in the field in which you are interested. Even if the person is a potential employer, it is best to phrase your request as if you were seeking information: "You might not be able to help me, but do you know someone I could talk to who could tell me more about what it is like to work in this field?" Being hungry gives one impression, being desperate quite another.

Keep in mind that networking is a two-way street. If you meet someone who has an opening that is not right for you, but you could recommend someone else, you have just added to your list two people who will be favorably disposed toward you in the future. Also, bear in mind that *you* can help people in *your* old field, thus adding to your own contacts list.

Networking is especially important to the self-employed or those who start their own businesses. Many people in this situation begin because they either recognize a potential market in a field that they are familiar with, or because full-time employment in this industry is no longer a possibility. Already being well-established in a field can help, but so can asking connections for potential work and generally making it known that you are ready, willing, and able to work. Working your professional connections, in many cases, is the *only* way to establish yourself. A freelancer's network, in many cases, is like a spider's web. The spider casts out many strands, since he or she never knows which one might land the next meal.

Dial-Up Help

In general, it is better to call contacts directly than to e-mail them. E-mails are easy for busy people to ignore or overlook, even if they do not mean to. Explain your situation as briefly as possible (see the discussion of the "elevator speech"), and ask if you could meet briefly, either at their office or at a neutral place such as a café. (Be sure that you pay the bill in such a situation—it is a way of showing you appreciate their time and effort.) If you get someone's voicemail, give your "elevator speech" and then say you will call back in a few days to follow up—and then do so. If you reach your contact directly and they are too busy to speak or meet with you, make a definite appointment to call back at a later date. Be persistent, but not annoying.

Once you have arranged a meeting, prep yourself. Look at industry publications both in print and online, as well as news reports (here, GoogleNews, which lets you search through online news reports, can be very handy). Having up-to-date information on industry trends shows that you are dedicated, knowledgeable, and focused. Having specific questions on employers and requests for suggestions will set you apart from the rest of the job-hunting pack. Knowing the score—for instance, asking about the value of one sort of certification instead of another—pegs you as an "insider," rather than a dilettante, someone whose name is worth remembering and passing along to a potential employer.

Finally, set the right mood. Here, a little self-hypnosis goes a long way: Look at yourself in the mirror, and tell yourself that you are an enthusiastic, committed professional. Mood affects confidence and performance. Discipline your mind so you keep your perspective and self-respect. Nobody wants to hire someone who comes across as insincere, tells a sob story, or is still in the doldrums of having lost their previous job. At the end of any networking meeting, ask for someone else who might be able to help you in your journey to finding a position in this field, either with information or a potential job opening.

Get a Lift

When you meet with a contact in person (as well as when you run into anyone by chance who may be able to help you), you need an "elevator speech" (so-named because it should be short enough to be delivered during an elevator ride from a ground level to a high floor). This is a summary in which, in less than two minutes, you give them a clear impression of who you are, where you come from, your experience and goals, and why you are on the path you are on. The motto above Plato's Academy holds true: Know Thyself (this is where our Career Compasses and guides will help you). A long and rambling "elevator story" will get you nowhere. Furthermore, be positive: Neither a sad-sack story nor a tirade explaining how everything that went wrong in your old job is someone else's fault will get you anywhere. However, an honest explanation of a less-than-fortunate circumstance, such as a decline in business forcing an office closure, needing to change residence to a place where you are not qualified to work in order to further your spouse's career, or needing to work fewer hours in order to care for an ailing family member, is only honest.

An elevator speech should show 1) you know the business involved; 2) you know the company; 3) you are qualified (here, try to relate your education and work experience to the new situation); and 4) you are goal-oriented, dependable, and hardworking. Striking a balance is important; you want to sound eager, but not overeager. You also want to show a steady work experience, but not that you have been so narrowly focused that you cannot adjust. Most important is emphasizing what you can do for the company. You will be surprised how much information you can include in two minutes. Practice this speech in front of a mirror until you have the key points down perfectly. It should sound natural, and you should come across as friendly, confident, and assertive. Finally, remember eye contact! Good eye contact needs to be part of your presentation, as well as your everyday approach when meeting potential employers and leads.

Get Your Résumé Ready

Everyone knows what a résumé is, but how many of us have really thought about how to put one together? Perhaps no single part of the job search is subject to more anxiety—or myths and misunderstandings—than this 8 ½-by-11-inch sheet of paper.

On the one hand, it is perfectly all right for someone—especially in certain careers, such as academia—to have a résumé that is more than one page. On the other hand, you do not need to tell a future employer *everything*. Trim things down to the most relevant; for a 40-year-old to mention an internship from two decades ago is superfluous. Likewise, do not include irrelevant jobs, lest you seem like a professional career-changer.

Tailor your descriptions of your former employment to the particular position you are seeking. This is not to say you should lie, but do make your experience more appealing. If the job you're looking for involves supervising other people, say if you have done this in the past; if it involves specific knowledge or capabilities, mention that you possess these qualities. In general, try to make your past experience seem similar to what you are seeking.

The standard advice is to put your Job Objective at the heading of the résumé. An alternative to this is a Professional Summary, which some recruiters and employers prefer. The difference is that a Job Objective mentions the position you are seeking, whereas a Professional Summary mentions your background (e.g. "Objective: To find a position as a sales representative in agribusiness machinery" versus "Experienced sales representative; strengths include background in agribusiness, as well as building team dynamics and market expansion"). Of course, it is easy to come up with two or three versions of the same document for different audiences.

The body of the résumé of an experienced worker varies a lot more than it does at the beginning of your career. You need not put your education or your job experience first; rather, your résumé should emphasize your strengths. If you have a master's degree in a related field, that might want to go before your unrelated job experience. Conversely, if too much education will harm you, you might want to bury that under the section on professional presentations you have given that show how good you are at communicating. If you are currently enrolled in a course or other professional development, be sure to note this (as well as your date of expected graduation). A résumé is a study of blurs, highlights, and jewels. You blur everything you must in order to fit the description of your experience to the job posting. You highlight what is relevant from each and any of your positions worth mentioning. The jewels are the little headers and such—craft them, since they are what is seen first.

You may also want to include professional organizations, work-related achievements, and special abilities, such as your fluency in a foreign language. Also mention your computer software qualifications and capabilities, especially if you are looking for work in a technological field or if you are an older job-seeker who might be perceived as behind the technology curve. Including your interests or family information might or might not be a good idea—no one really cares about your bridge club, and in fact they might worry that your marathon training might take away from your work commitments, but, on the other hand, mentioning your golf handicap or three children might be a good idea if your potential employer is an avid golfer or is a family woman herself.

You can either include your references or simply note, "References available upon request." However, be sure to ask your references' permission to use their names and alert them to the fact that they may be contacted before you include them on your résumé! Be sure to include name, organization, phone number, and e-mail address for each contact.

Today, word processors make it easy to format your résumé. However, beware of prepackaged résumé "wizards"—they do not make you stand out in the crowd. Feel free to strike out on your own, but remember the most important thing in formatting a résumé is consistency. Unless you have a background in typography, do not get too fancy. Finally, be sure to have someone (or several people!) read your résumé over for you.

For more information on résumé writing, check out Web sites such as http://www.résumé.monster.com.

Craft Your Cover Letter

It is appropriate to include a cover letter with your résumé. A cover letter lets you convey extra information about yourself that does not fit or is not always appropriate in your résumé, such as why you are no longer working in your original field of employment. You can and should also mention the name of anyone who referred you to the job. You can go into some detail about the reason you are a great match, given the job description. Also address any questions that might be raised in the potential employer's mind (for instance, a gap in employment). Do not, however, ramble on. Your cover letter should stay focused on your goal: To offer a strong, positive impression of yourself and persuade the hiring manager that you are worth an interview. Your cover letter gives you a chance to stand out from the other applicants and sell yourself. In fact, according to a CareerBuilder.

com survey, 23 percent of hiring managers say a candidate's ability to relate his or her experience to the job at hand is a top hiring consideration.

Even if you are not a great writer, you can still craft a positive yet concise cover letter in three paragraphs: An introduction containing the specifics of the job you are applying for; a summary of why you are a good fit for the position and what you can do for the company; and a closing with a request for an interview, contact information, and thanks. Remember to vary the structure and tone of your cover letter—do not begin every sentence with "I."

Ace Your Interview

In truth, your interview begins well before you arrive. Be sure to have read up well on the company and its industry. Use Web sites and magazines—http://www.hoovers.com offers free basic business information, and trade magazines deliver both information and a feel for the industries they cover. Also, do not neglect talking to people in your circle who might know about trends in the field. Leave enough time to digest the information so that you can give some independent thought to the company's history and prospects. You don't need to be an expert when you arrive to be interviewed; but you should be comfortable. The most important element of all is to be poised and relaxed during the interview itself. Preparation and practice can help a lot.

Be sure to develop well-thought-through answers to the following, typical interview openers and standard questions.

☞ Tell me about yourself. (Do not complain about how unsatisfied you were in your former career, but give a brief summary of your applicable background and interest in the particular job area.) If there is a basis to it, emphasize how much you love to work and how you are a team player.

☞ Why do you want this job? (Speak from the brain, and the heart—of course you want the money, but say a little here about what you find interesting about the field and the company's role in it.)

☞ What makes you a good hire? (Remember here to connect the company's needs and your skill set. Ultimately, your selling points probably come down to one thing: you will make your employer money. You want the prospective hirer to see that your skills are valuable not to the world in general but to this specific company's bottom line. What can you do for them?)

☞ What led you to leave your last job? (If you were fired, still try to say something positive, such as, "The business went through a challenging time, and some of the junior marketing people were let go.")

Practice answering these and other questions, and try to be genuinely positive about yourself, and patient with the process. Be secure but not cocky; don't be shy about forcing the focus now and then on positive contributions you have made in your working life—just be specific. As with the elevator speech, practice in front of the mirror.

A couple pleasantries are as natural a way as any to start the actual interview, but observe the interviewer closely for any cues to fall silent and formally begin. Answer directly; when in doubt, finish your phrase and look to the interviewer. Without taking command, you can always ask, "Is there more you would like to know?" Your attentiveness will convey respect. Let your personality show too—a positive attitude and a grounded sense of your abilities will go a long way to getting you considered. During the interview, keep your cell phone off and do not look at your watch. Toward the end of your meeting, you may be asked whether you have any questions. It is a good idea to have one or two in mind. A few examples follow:

☞ "What makes your company special in the field?"

☞ "What do you consider the hardest part of this position?"

☞ "Where are your greatest opportunities for growth?"

☞ "Do you know when you might need anything further from me?"

Leave discussion of terms for future conversations. Make a cordial, smooth exit.

Remember to Follow Up

Send a thank-you note. Employers surveyed by CareerBuilder.com in 2005 said it matters. About 15 percent said they would not hire someone who did not follow up with a thanks. And almost 33 percent would think less of a candidate. The form of the note does not much matter—if you know a manager's preference, use it. Otherwise, just be sure to follow up.

Winning an Offer

A job offer can feel like the culmination of a long and difficult struggle. So naturally, when you hear them, you may be tempted to jump at the offer. Don't. Once an employer wants you, he or she will usually give you a chance to consider the offer. This is the time to discuss terms of employment, such as vacation, overtime, and benefits. A little effort now can be well worth it in the future. Be sure to do a check of prevailing salaries for your field and area before signing on. Web sites for this include Payscale.com, Salary.com, and Salaryexpert.com. If you are thinking about asking for better or different terms from what the prospective employer offered, rest assured—that's how business gets done; and it may just burnish the positive impression you have already made.

Index

A

AED. *See* automated external defibrillator
AEMA. *See* American Equipment Managers
  Association
age group landmarks
  athletic director, 43–45
  athletic trainer, 26–27
  coaches/sports instructors, 7–8
  fitness worker, 35
  scout, 79–80
  sports agent, 53–54
  sports equipment manager, 61–62
  sports event manager, 88
  sports facility manager, 70
  umpires/referees, 17–18
American Alliance for Health, Physical
  Education Recreation and Dance, 9
American Baseball Coaches Association, 9
American College of Sports Medicine, 36
American Council on Exercise, 36
American Equipment Managers Association
  (AEMA), 58, 61, 62
American Independent Business Alliance,
  101
American Small Business League, 101
Amplify Sports and Entertainment, 88
athletic director, xii, 38–45
  age group landmarks, 43–45
  career compasses, 38
  essential gear, 39, 40
  field notes, 44–45
  job description, 38–41
  job prospects, 40
  resources, 45
  skills/qualifications, 41–42
  training/education, 40–41, 43
  transition expedition, 42–43

athletics, women in, xv, 39
athletic trainer, xii–xiii, 20–27
  age group landmarks, 26–27
  background/related work experience, 23
  career compasses, 20
  certification, xiii, 27
  essential gear, 21, 22, 26
  field notes, 25
  job description, 20–23
  job prospects, 23
  resources, 26, 27
  salaries/wages, 23
  skills/qualifications, 21, 23
  training/education, 21
  transition expedition, 24–26
automated external defibrillator (AED), 26

B

background/related work experience, xii
  athletic trainer, 23
  coaches/sports instructors, 6
  fitness worker, 32
  scout, 76
  sports agent, 49
  sports event manager, 87
  sports facility manager, 68
Board of Certification, 27
bookkeeping, 97–98
Bureau of Labor Statistics, vi, vii, 3–4, 50
business, starting own, 91–101
  bookkeeping for, 97–98
  building, 99–100
  employer in, being, 98–99
  financial issues in, 96–97
  incorporation of, 94–95
  legal issues in, 95–96
  partnership in, 93–94
  plan, 91–93